170 THO

D0765971

easy

Mel Thompson

flash.

Hodder Education
338 Euston Road, London NW1 3BH.

Hodder Education is an Hachette UK company

First published in UK 2011 by Hodder Education.

This edition published 2011.

Copyright © Mel Thompson

British Library Cataloguing in Publication Data: a catalogue record for this title
is available from the British Library.

10 9 8 7 6 5 4 3 2 1

The publisher has used its best endeavours to ensure that any website
addresses referred to in this book are correct and active at the time of going
to press. However, the publisher and the author have no responsibility for the
websites and can make no guarantee that a site will remain live or that the
content will remain relevant, decent or appropriate.

The publisher has made every effort to mark as such all words which it
believes to be trademarks. The publisher should also like to make it clear that
the presence of a word in the book, whether marked or unmarked, in no way
affects its legal status as a trademark.

Every reasonable effort has been made by the publisher to trace the copyright
holders of material in this book. Any errors or omissions should be notified in
writing to the publisher, who will endeavour to rectify the situation for any
reprints and future editions.

Hachette UK's policy is to use papers that are natural, renewable and
recyclable products and made from wood grown in sustainable forests.
The logging and manufacturing processes are expected to conform to the
environmental regulations of the country of origin.

www.hoddereducation.co.uk

Typeset by MPS Limited, a Macmillan Company.
Printed in Great Britain by CPI Cox & Wyman, Reading.

Contents

1

introduction

Ethics, or 'moral philosophy', is about thinking through issues of right or wrong. It examines the moral choices that people make, what they are based on and how they may be justified. Unlike 'descriptive ethics', which simply looks at how people actually behave, 'normative ethics' (with which this book is concerned) considers the norms and principles that guide – or should guide – action.

When applied to society as a whole, ethics moves into the sphere of political philosophy and law, but this book concentrates on moral arguments that apply to the actions of individuals and the choices they make.

We start by recognizing that facts alone are not enough to distinguish right from wrong – just because everybody does something, that doesn't make it right – and that, in order to be morally responsible for our actions, we have to have a measure of freedom, for it makes no sense to be blamed for something about which we have no choice.

> **'What should I do?'**
> **'How do I know what is right?'**

These basic questions are the starting point for ethical debate, for ethics is about moral choices. It is about the values that lie behind them, the reasons people give for them and the language they use to describe them. It is about innocence and guilt, right and wrong, and what it means to live a good or bad life. It is about the dilemmas of life, death, sex, violence and money. It explores human virtues and vices, rights and duties.

Babies are lucky. They feel hungry, or dirty, or wet, and just scream until someone figures out what is wrong and gives them what they need. They do not have the intellectual ability to question how they got into their particular mess, or the steps they need to take to get out of it. They are not morally responsible.

One essential difference between a baby and a mature adult is that the adult recognizes when there is a problem to be overcome, or a difficult choice to be made, takes action and then accepts responsibility. **Ethics is the rational discussion of that process.**

What makes something moral?

Many choices are a straightforward matter of personal preference, and the actions that spring from them are neither moral nor immoral. They only become the subject of moral debate because of the intentions behind them, their results, and the values – of society or of the individual – that they reflect.

Actions can be divided into three categories:

* **moral** – if they reflect a person's values and those of society
* **immoral** – if they go against a person's (or society's) values
* **amoral** – if they do not reflect choices based on values or social norms.

Of course, an individual may think that something is moral even if the rest of society thinks it immoral. Doing something immoral is not the same thing as breaking the law. Actions can be moral but illegal, or immoral but legal.

Whether you think an action is moral or immoral will depend on your values and the ethical arguments you use to decide what is right. How many actions or choices are moral and how many relegated to the general 'amoral' category, will depend on your moral sensitivity, the range of values to which you consciously subscribe, and whether you belong to a society which operates by definite rules and values.

Issues that are morally significant usually have to do with relationships, agreements between parties, intentions and possible outcomes. The moral status of an action may therefore depend less on what actually happens than on the intention of the person who performs it and the appropriateness of what is done.

Example

A masked stranger makes you lie on a table, drugs you into unconsciousness, takes out a sharp knife and slices into your naked body. Is the action moral, immoral or amoral?

At this point you might well want to know if the person with the knife is a competent surgeon or a student of the Marquis de Sade!

A description of the action itself is not necessarily the best guide to its moral consequences. You might therefore ask:
   * Is this a qualified surgeon?
   * Have I consented to this operation?
   * Is it likely to benefit me?
   * Have the implications of it been explained to me?
   * If the person is not a surgeon, do I want him or her to continue? (It might, after all, be emergency, and an unqualified surgeon might be better than none.)
   * What are his or her motives for doing this operation? (Money? Genuine altruism?)
   * If for motives other than these (e.g. sexual gratification), would I still want him or her to continue, if I believed that it would benefit me?

Facts alone do not decide whether something is right or wrong: 'People are dying of starvation' is not a moral statement. But if you add '... and you are doing nothing to help', then it becomes a moral issue if the person addressed is in a position to help, but does not do so.

In other words, for an issue or an action to be described as moral, it needs to take into consideration human choices and intentions and the values that lie behind them. Simply presenting facts, however important they may be, is not the same thing as framing an ethical argument.

In practical terms, the study of ethics can offer two things. First of all, it helps one to appreciate the moral choices that people make, and to evaluate the justification they give for those choices. But secondly, it involves a reflective sharpening of one's own moral awareness – a conscious examination of values and principles, of how these have influenced one's life, and (more importantly) of how they can be used to shape the future.

Free to choose?

Nobody is completely free to do anything that he or she may wish. Freedom is limited in different ways:

* I may decide that I would like to launch myself into the air, spread my arms and fly. I may have dreamed of doing so. I may have a passion for Superman films, and feel certain that in some way it should be possible. But my physical body is, and will always be, incapable of unaided flight. To overcome that limitation, I must resort to technology.
* I may wish to be a famous and highly talented artist, musician or gymnast, but my freedom is again limited. It may not be physically impossible for me to achieve these things, but it requires such a level of experience, training and natural ability, that my chances of achieving what I want are severely restricted.
* I may wish to go to London and parade myself naked before Buckingham Palace. There is no physical limitation to inhibit me and no great skill required, but I am likely to be arrested if I do so.

These are examples of limitation to actual freedom. Whether by physical laws, natural abilities, or legal or social restraints, we are all limited in what we can do.

If I am to make a moral choice, I must be free to do, or not to do, the thing in question. It cannot be morally wrong not to fly, because I am unable to do so. On the other hand, walking about naked in public could become a moral issue – if it were argued that I would give offence by doing so – because it would be something that I had chosen to do and could have refused to do had I considered it wrong.

Determinism

Science is based on the observation of natural events and their causes, and from the resulting information is able to develop theories by which events may be predicted.

You look up and say 'I think it is going to rain.' You do not thereby imply that the weather has a personality, and that you guess that it has decided to enjoy a little precipitation. Rather, you make a comment based on the clouds, wind, dampness in the air, and on your observation of similar things leading to rain on previous occasions.

* The falling of rain is determined absolutely by certain atmospheric conditions.
* The fact that you may be inaccurate in predicting those conditions, and therefore the coming of rain, does not detract from the fundamentally determined nature of that event.
* Given certain conditions, it will rain; without them, it will not: the weather is determined. Its absolute prediction is theoretically possible, even if practically difficult.

The prediction of rain is possible because it is recognized that all physical phenomena are causally connected. Everything from the weather to the electrical impulses within human brains can be explained in terms of physical laws. This is **determinism.**

There is a general acceptance that all events (including human action) may be explained in terms of prior events, which are considered to have caused them. And in the case of human action, this may be explained (at least to some extent) in terms of the effect of environment or upbringing on the individual, along with all the other physical constraints that limit our action.

Example

A car swerves across the road and collides with a tree, killing the driver.

Why did the car swerve? Did a tyre burst? If so, how worn was it? Was there a fault in its manufacture? Was there a steering fault in the car? If so, was there a design fault? (Accidents in which the harm done is made worse through a design fault can lead to the manufacturer being prosecuted, as having contributed to that overall harm.)

What if you trace everything back, from the skill of the driver, to the food that he or she has been eating (was the driver faint? sick? drunk?), to whether the tree should have been planted so close to the road? The driver may have had control over some of these things, but not over others. Yet everything that has ever happened contributes in some way to each event. Is anyone to blame? What if the road had not been built? What if cars had not been invented?

If we had total knowledge, everything would be seen to fit a seamless pattern of cause and effect. But those experiencing that event (the driver before dying; those who knew him, or witnessed the crash) will see it differently. They may wish that other decisions had been made. They may feel guilty, saying 'if only ...'. There is an inescapable sense that events are influenced by human choice. Without that sense, the issue of moral responsibility would not arise.

We may be socially or psychologically predisposed to act in a certain way, as a result of upbringing or environment. Our genetic make-up may give a predisposition to violence, depression, schizophrenia or our particular sexual orientation. Does that imply that we should take no responsibility for these things?

If a direct causal link could be shown, then the case for determinism in these areas of life would be strengthened. On the other hand, whereas physical traits (e.g. the colour of one's eyes) are 100 per cent due to heredity, studies of twins have suggested that behavioural factors, such as homosexuality, can have a heredity factor as low as 31 per cent. This illustrates what common sense would suggest, that there are other factors as well as our genes that influence our behaviour. This does not, however, disprove a claim that everything is determined. It merely shows that no one factor alone can be shown to determine the final result, but taken together they do so, each contributing something to the determinist equation.

These things may influence our freedom, but not necessarily the *freedom of our will*. We may *believe* we are free to choose, even if the psychologist, sociologist or behavioural geneticist claims to know better.

Freedom and the State

In the discussion so far, we have been looking in a rather abstract way at whether or not a person is free to decide how to act. But in practical terms, even if we feel that we are free, we are actually constrained by the legal and social rules of the society within which we live.

If we are caught breaking a law, we are punished. If we are not caught, we may still feel guilty. Freedom is not simply a matter of biology, but of social and political life. If a person joins in a demonstration in favour of greater freedom, he or she is unlikely to be concerned about whether there can be a scientific explanation for each muscular action as he or she walks forward; but more likely to be campaigning for social or political freedom and restoration to the individual of choices presently prohibited by some authority.

But should every individual be free to choose exactly how he or she should live? In any particular country, people need to decide whether they will all drive on the right or the left, otherwise there will be chaos on the roads. Common sense dictates that an individual should not have the freedom to drive on the other side. But should everyone automatically have a right to take part in the democratic process to select a government? The answer to this is not so clear, because the results are less obvious.

Plato, for example, (in *The Republic* book IX) argued that most ordinary people did not have a strongly rational nature, and therefore needed to be constrained in what they did by being ruled by those who were naturally more rational. Philosophers alone, he thought, would have sufficient detachment to be able to legislate for the good of society as a whole. In that book, Plato presents the different arguments in the form of a debate between individuals. One of these, Thrasymachus, argues that laws are always made in the interests of the ruling class, and Glaucon comments that basically everyone would like to act from purely selfish motives, although all would suffer as a result of the ensuing chaos. Both of these views of human and social motives find echoes throughout the history of ethics.

How much freedom does morality need?

* It does not need us to be absolutely free.
* It does not even need us to be free of things that influence our moral choice (indeed, the more sensitive a person is, the more he or she is aware of such influences).

However, morality requires that:
* Whatever may happen in terms of the mechanical side of life, we experience ourselves as free agents who can make genuine choices.
* Even if I admit the existence of external moral pressure to conform to some rule, I am acting morally only if I am in a position to think about and either conform to or reject the pressures on me.

* Other people, observing my behaviour, may come to conclusions about my personality and general attitude towards life. Having done so, they may predict accurately what I will do in any given circumstance. That element of prediction, however accurate, does not in itself prevent me from experiencing myself as making a free choice.

Free will

It is important to make the distinction between freedom in general and freedom of the will. I may look at various options, and think that I am free to choose between them. Someone who knows me well may, on hearing my decision, say 'I just knew you would choose to do that!' Is it possible for my will to be free, for it to be possible for me to weigh up all the factors involved and come to a genuinely free choice, and yet for someone else to be able to predict accurately what I will do? (And it will not be any use changing my mind at the last minute, or acting out of character, because those things too could be predicted.)

There is something intensely irritating about people saying that they know exactly what you will freely choose to do. This is because, in the moment of choice, we experience freedom. Robots and computers may be totally predictable, but most humans are convinced that they themselves are not.

Consider the following cases of murder:

1 A thief shoots and kills a bank clerk in the course of a raid.
2 A husband or wife kills his or her partner after years of provocation and unhappiness.
3 A young man rapes and kills a girl whom he has not met before, on account of his particularly violent sexual urges.
4 A psychopath, unwisely released from a secure hospital to live in the community, kills someone for no apparent reason, does not attempt to conceal the crime, and shows no remorse when apprehended and charged with murder.

All four have killed another human being. But are they all equally guilty in a moral sense? Do any of them have genuine grounds for having the charge of murder reduced to that of manslaughter, for example?

1 It is assumed that the bank robber freely chooses to carry a weapon. Even if the actual shot were the result of being startled by a sudden movement, for example, that does not detract significantly from the general view that his act was murder, because he exercised freedom of the will in deciding to carry a loaded weapon.

2 With domestic murder, there may be a significant element of provocation. In that case, especially if the murder takes place in the course of a heated argument, it might be argued that the victim contributed to the situation that brought about the crime, or that (if sufficiently provoked) the murder took place while the person concerned was temporarily deranged. He or she might be charged with manslaughter on the grounds of diminished responsibility.

3 The issue in the case of the sexual murder is one of the freedom of the murderer to decide whether or not to act on his sexual impulses. If it can be shown that the condition is such that the person is not in control of himself or herself in certain situations, then psychiatric reports would be relevant evidence to bring before the court.

4 The psychopath is not in control of his or her actions, and does not respond to the normal inhibitions and rational constraints that apply to those who are sane.

The psychopath is certainly not free to choose how to act. But what of the person with an uncontrollable sexual urge? Or the provoked wife? In each case we have to examine personal, psychological and social factors.

Suppose it is shown that there is more vandalism in areas of high unemployment. Does that imply that those who are unemployed are less able to choose freely what they do? Are social pressures enough to justify actions that can be regarded by other people as morally wrong?

In extreme situations, the pressure on a person is so great, that he or she feels that all freedom to choose what to do has been taken away. Unlike the psychopath, he or she is fully aware of the implications of what is done, but the need to act in that particular way is overwhelming. This is loss of freedom, but not freedom of the will. An extreme example of this is where death is the only alternative to a particular course of action.

Overall, we need to be aware that nobody is completely free, for we all act within physical, emotional, social, legal or political constraints. On the other hand, such constraints still leave scope for freedom of the will; if we make choices, if we decide whether or not to obey a rule, we are exercising what feels like personal freedom. The key question is whether that experience of freedom is real or illusory. And if it is illusory – if it can be shown that everything is determined and explicable – does that take away all personal responsibility?

what do we mean?

To make moral statements, or engage in ethical debate, we need to use language. This chapter therefore explores the different forms of ethical language, in order to clarify what part each has to play.

We shall look at descriptive, normative and meta-ethics, noting what they do and their limitations, before moving on to examine two ethical theories that attempted to respond to the challenge of those who claimed that moral language was meaningless because it was not based on evidence – emotivism and prescriptivism.

Yet philosophers from Plato and Aristotle onwards have sought to find an objective and universal basis for moral claims, based on features of social or natural life. So we are still left with the question of how to relate such facts of life (the 'is') with our sense of morality (the 'ought'). We therefore take a look at David Hume's warning about moving from the one to the other.

In ethics, three different kinds of language are used. We need to distinguish them carefully, and know which we are using at any one time, if we are not to become confused.

Descriptive ethics

This is the most straightforward form of ethics. It consists of descriptions of the way in which people live, and the moral choices they make. It simply presents facts. Two simple examples of descriptive ethics follow.

Most car crime is carried out by young men in areas of high unemployment.

The actual information may be correct or incorrect. It can be checked by referring to police records and employment statistics. But notice that the statement does not make any moral claim about youth and crime, nor does it say whether unemployment is a good or bad thing. It does not even make (although it may be taken to imply) a connection between crime and unemployment.

Muslim men may marry up to four wives, provided that they are able to provide for them and treat them equally.

Again, this makes no moral judgement, nor does it enquire whether it is possible to treat wives equally. It simply states the fact about what is permitted within a certain religious and cultural setting.

Normative ethics

Ethics is concerned with ideas about what is right, about justice, about how people should live. It examines the choices people make, and the values and reasoning that lie behind them. This is sometimes called 'substantive' or 'normative' ethics. Almost all moral argument, when it is concerned with the rights or wrongs of particular issues, is of this kind.

It is always wrong to steal.

This is a normative statement. It can be challenged by using another normative statement, for example, 'No, I think it is right to steal on some occasions.' What you cannot do is challenge a normative statement by using a descriptive one. So a person who responds by saying 'but everyone around here steals if they get a chance' is not actually countering the claim that it is wrong to steal. Everyone may do something, but that does not make it right.

Descriptive ethics is about facts, **normative ethics** is about values. Both are needed, but it is essential to realize that you cannot argue directly from the one to the other: **you cannot get an 'ought' from an 'is'**.

Meta-ethics

It is also possible to stand back from moral statements and ask:

* What does it mean to say that something is right or wrong?
* Are there any objective criteria by which I can assess moral statements?
* What is moral language? Is it a statement about facts of any kind?
* Does a moral statement simply express a person's wishes or hopes about what should happen?
* In what sense can a moral statement be said to be either true or false?

Questions like these are not concerned with the content of moral discourse, but with its meaning. This fits in very closely with much twentieth-century philosophy, which explored the nature of language and the way in which statements can be shown to be true or false. Looking at moral statements in this way is called **meta-ethics**.

Notice that each kind of ethical language has its dangers:

* The danger of descriptive ethics is that facts will be mistaken for values.
* The danger of normative ethics is that, in arguing that something is right or wrong, one may end up preaching rather than informing, recommending one particular course of action rather than setting out all the possibilities,

consequences and values, and then allowing a person to make an informed and thoughtful choice.
* The danger of meta-ethics is that one may become so obsessed with the issue of meaning that it becomes impossible to offer any practical guidance for the difficult choices that people have to make.

Defining key terms

Moral language uses certain words, without which normative ethics would not make sense. One of these is the word **ought** – expressing a sense of moral obligation. Another is **justice** – examining the rights of individuals in society and the way in which they 'ought' to treat one another. The most basic word, however, is **good**. An action is judged 'right' or 'wrong' depending on whether or not it is a 'good' or 'bad' thing to do. Before we can talk about moral values we need to know what we mean by this term. Actions cannot be right or wrong unless we know what we mean by goodness. But can it be defined?

You could try to define 'good' in absolute terms (that something is good in itself) or in relative terms (that it is good in its particular context). You can also define it in terms of what it can achieve – so an action is 'good' (and right) if the results of that action are 'good'. This would be a utilitarian assessment, as we shall see later. But we are still using the word 'good' and are therefore no nearer a definition.

Aristotle argued that something was 'good' if it fulfilled its purpose. On this theory, a good knife is one that cuts well; a good plant is one that grows strong and healthy. This formed the basis of what is called the **natural law** approach to ethics. According to this, everything has a natural purpose in life, and actions are right or wrong depending on whether or not they contribute to the fulfilling of that purpose.

A religious believer may say that 'good' is what God approves, and take a particular revelation (e.g. the Bible) as the norm for understanding goodness. Another may take a particular experience, or the life of a religious leader, as the starting point for understanding the 'good' life. The meaning of the word good will therefore depend, in part, on the source of the values that are called 'good', and that is not something on which everyone will automatically agree.

Some theories

Ethics is concerned with what moral language means, what it does, and how it may be verified. We shall therefore look briefly at some theories about moral language.

Emotivism

In the early part of the twentieth century there developed an approach to language that is generally known as **logical positivism**.

It was an attempt to break down language into its simplest components and examine their meaning. This movement, inspired by the early work of Wittgenstein (as seen in his *Tractatus Logico Philosophicus*), is represented by the Vienna Circle of philosophers (including, for example, Carnap and Schlick) and became widely known through the publication in 1936 of A. J. Ayer's controversial book *Language Truth and Logic*.

The details of this approach need not detain us, except to say that it held that all meaningful propositions could be divided into two categories – **tautologies** (statements that are true by definition, e.g. all bachelors are unmarried) and **empirical statements of fact**, verified by observation. If a statement was not a tautology, and could not be shown to relate to externally perceived facts, then it was said to be meaningless. Now, on that basis, moral statements are meaningless, as they are neither statements of fact nor definitions. If my saying that you 'should' do something is neither a statement of fact nor a tautology, what is it? One answer to this is termed **emotivism**.

Ayer suggested that a moral statement is a kind of command:

The exhortations to moral virtue are not propositions at all, but ejaculations or commands which are designed to provoke the reader to action of a certain sort. Accordingly, they do not belong to any branch of philosophy or science.

For Ayer, moral judgements expressed the feelings of the speaker. Carnap (a member of the Vienna Circle) also thought that moral statements were commands (if I say 'This is the right thing to do, I really mean 'do this!') while Schlick thought that they were rules. Bertrand Russell argued that differences in values (and therefore differences in the moral statements that are based on them) are not a matter of facts, but of taste.

C. L. Stevenson, in *Ethics and Language*, 1947, claimed that, once you strip the supposed facts away from moral statements, they are revealed for what they really are: expressions of a person's own preferences and emotions. **To say that something is right is really just another way of saying that I approve of it.** Stevenson therefore argued that 'good' was a **persuasive definition**. He was less concerned with what moral statements meant in themselves, and more with what they were for. **A statement has an emotive meaning if it is intended to produce a response in the person who hears it.**

There are two main criticisms of this approach:

* A moral argument is not really judged according to the response it evokes, but on whether its claims are valid. Morality is not just about emotions, but may be discussed rationally.

* To claim something is right or wrong is to make a policy statement. If I claim my moral judgements are universal (they should apply to everyone) they cannot be based on feelings, for I cannot say what others should feel, nor can I know what I will feel on other occasions.

Prescriptivism

Whereas the **emotivist** asks what sort of effect a moral statement aims to have, a **prescriptivist** is more concerned about what is happening when someone actually makes a moral statement.

R. M. Hare (in *The Language of Morals*, 1952, and *Freedom and Reason*, 1963) is the best-known representative of this approach. He asks about what a moral statement is meant to do, and concludes that a moral statement is 'prescribing' a course of action – recommending that something should be done, rather than just expressing the feelings of the speaker.

This may sound similar in practice to a **command**, but there is a difference. If I see someone about to steal a car and I shout out 'Stop that!' I am referring to that single incident. I am not suggesting that stopping doing things is a general principle on which I expect the person to base his life! On the other hand, if I say 'It is wrong to steal!' I am giving a piece of advice that can apply to future situations as well.

Naturalism and metaphysical ethics

Reading Plato's *Republic*, or Aristotle's *Nicomachean Ethics*, we get the very definite idea that, in spite of the various views that are put forward and examined, there is ultimately a rational basis for the idea of goodness and justice – arising from the nature of human life, or the needs of a society to organize itself in a harmonious way.

The implication of this is that there is an objective basis for ethics. On the other hand, some of the theories put forward in this chapter may suggest that there is no objective truth in ethics, but that everything centres on the wishes or feelings of the person who makes the moral statement. This 'ethical subjectivism' may seem appropriate for a society that has no single religious, social, political or cultural base, for people differ from one another so greatly that it is unlikely that they would share the same values, or choose to act in the same way.

However, when it comes to moral issues, people try to persuade others about how they should behave. They argue as though there were some objective truth about which different people could in principle agree.

This situation gives rise to two other theories about ethical language. **Naturalistic ethics** is the term used for the attempt to explain a set of moral terms from the facts of human life. It is the positive side of what G. E. Moore criticized as the 'naturalistic fallacy' – the attempt to derive an 'ought' from an 'is'. By contrast, **metaphysical ethics** insists that morality should be valued in itself, and should be related to our understanding of the world and of our place within it. It points out that moral choices are related to our general understanding of life, and the value that we find in it: in other words, to our 'metaphysics'.

An interesting exposition of this approach was given by Iris Murdoch in her book *Metaphysics and a Guide to Morals* (Penguin, 1994), where she points out that the moral choices people make in times of crisis are based on the values that they gradually build up in their habitual way of dealing with the world. Hence, we should not separate off the moment of moral choice from the rest of our experience of life and our interpretation of it. We make ourselves what we are, and our choices follow from that.

Summary of theories

* **Intuitionism** – one just instinctively knows when something is right!
* **Emotivism** – one uses moral statements to express feelings, and influence the feelings of others.
* **Prescriptivism** – one uses moral statements to 'prescribe' a general course of action.
* **Naturalism** – relating moral statements to particular features of the world and of social relationships.
* **Metaphysical ethics** – relating moral statements to a general understanding of the world, its meaning and its values.

Now it is clear that, when we use moral language, we may be doing a combination of some or all of these things. We may speak about something being 'good' without knowing how to define what we mean by that word. We may speak out because we want to express our emotions. We may want to recommend a course of action. We may also feel convinced that there are objective grounds for saying that something is right or wrong.

'Is' and 'ought'

David Hume pointed out that those who write on religion or morality tend to slip from matters of fact to matters of value:

*In every system of morality, which I have hitherto met with,
I have always remarked, that the author proceeds for some
time in the ordinary way of reasoning, and establishes the
being of a God, or makes observations concerning human
affairs; when of a sudden I am surprised to find, that instead
of the usual copulations of propositions, is and is not, I meet
with no proposition that is not connected with an ought, or
an ought not. This change is imperceptible; but is, however,
of the last consequence. For as this ought, or ought not,
expresses some new relation or affirmation, it is necessary
that is should be observed and explained; and at the same
time that a reason should be given, for what seems altogether
inconceivable, how this new relation can be a deduction from
others, which are entirely different from it.*

(*A Treatise on Human Nature*, 1738)

Hume, here as elsewhere, delights in debunking traditional
religious and moral arguments. But he highlights a feature of
moral argument that is absolutely crucial, and which links with our
discussion of the nature of religious language.

The logical positivists argued that moral statements were
meaningless, since they were neither tautologies nor matters
that could be proved true or false with reference to evidence.
We looked at the reactions to this claim – principally in pointing to
the emotive and prescriptive approaches to understanding what
moral language was about. In effect, the logical positivists were
restating Hume's point. Although based on facts, moral language
goes beyond them. In the crudest sense this is simply the 'just
because everyone else does it, does not make it right' argument.

To what extent, then, can moral judgements be based on facts?
If facts have to be interpreted, or if something more is needed
before we can move from saying 'is' to saying 'ought', then we need
to make clear what that extra is. This issue is illustrated most clearly
by the 'natural law' approach to ethics, to which we now turn.

3

is it natural?

So far we have considered what it means for something to be moral, whether we have sufficient freedom to take responsibility for what we do, and what it means to make a moral statement. But moral statements, even if they express a personal preference or recommend a course of action, make claims about 'right' and 'wrong'. How can these be justified?

In this and the following three chapters we shall be looking attempts to find a rational and objective basis for moral judgements. The first of these – the theory of natural law – claims that nature, interpreted by human reason, shows that everything has a particular essence or purpose, the fulfilling of which is the 'good' to which it should aim.

Developed in the thirteenth century by Aquinas, and central to much Catholic moral thinking, the natural law argument can be traced back to the work of the ancient Greek philosopher Aristotle.

Aristotle distinguished between efficient causes and final causes: an **efficient cause** is what gets things done, a **final cause** is the purpose or intended end product. A child grows up to be an adult. Aristotle would say that an efficient cause of the child's growth is food and drink, but the final cause is the adult into which the child is growing. Similarly, if I take a piece of wood and carve it into a statue, the efficient cause is the knife that I use, but the final cause is the image that I seek to create.

On this theory, everything (both every object and every action) has some final meaning and purpose (its 'final cause') – its essential nature and place within the overall scheme of things – and this is what determines its 'good'.

Aquinas used Aristotle's ideas to argue that the world was created by God, and that everything should therefore have God's ultimate purpose as its final 'end' or 'good'. To understand God's will for it, and therefore what is 'right' for it, you only have to look at the purpose for which it has been made. A good knife is one that cuts well: that is what it is designed to do. But how do you decide what is a good human life?

Aquinas argued that everything had its proper 'end', as part of God's providential ordering of the world, but humankind was special in that it was also given reason and freedom. Humans could therefore understand and choose whether or not to follow their proper 'end'. This he called 'natural law' – the rational understanding and following of God's final purpose.

Some features of 'natural law'

* The term 'natural law' should not be used simply to refer to the laws of nature, which form the basis of science. It is the result of applying reason to what happens in nature.
* As traditionally presented, the 'natural law' theory of ethics is based on the idea that God creates everything with a particular purpose in mind, and that people are therefore required to understand it and act accordingly. Hence, its authority tends to be religious.

* 'Natural law' can be examined quite apart from its religious interpretation, as a rational theory relating behaviour to the basic features of human life, its place within the world, and the basic requirements for its survival.
* It has the advantage that, once a 'final cause' is established, it may be applied to all people at all times. A natural law theory need take little account of prevailing social attitudes.
* It is not based on personal preferences, nor on guessing what the results of an action might be in terms of the happiness or otherwise of those involved – it is simply based on an examination of rational purpose. Potentially, it is a very 'clear-cut' ethical theory.

Natural law supports other general views of moral behaviour. Aquinas (in *Summa Theologiae*) presented the four cardinal virtues – prudence, justice, fortitude and temperance (which had been used as a basis for morality by the Stoics) – as fundamental qualities of the moral life. The opposite of these virtues are the seven capital vices (often called the 'seven deadly sins'), which are pride, avarice, lust, envy, gluttony, anger and sloth. From a traditional standpoint of belief in God, one might say that the former allow a human being to fulfil his or her potential as a human being as intended by God, whereas the latter frustrate that intention.

But the issue of what is 'natural' is wider than Aquinas' theory, for 'natural law' is essentially about finding the rational principles on which the world is made and which may therefore guide action. But many actions that may be described as natural are irrational and destructive, so further questions need to be asked.

How do you decide what is 'natural'?

Science bases its 'laws of nature' on observation, and they claim to be no more than an interpretation of the best available evidence. If something is observed that does not fit in with an established law, then either the observation is inaccurate, or another (as yet unknown) law has unexpectedly come into operation.

Our understanding of the way in which nature works is therefore constantly being modified.

If this also applies to 'natural law' as an ethical theory, then we cannot establish fixed criteria for right and wrong – which was the aim of Aquinas and others who followed this line of thought – because our concept of what is natural, and therefore of 'final causes', will always be open to modification.

Example

Natural law is about what life *should* be like, given a rational and purposeful creation, but that may not be what life is *actually* like.

It is natural for someone who is seriously ill to die. Does that mean that one should not interfere with the natural course of a disease by giving medicine?

In the natural world, the strongest animals often mate with as many sexual partners as they can, fighting off weaker rivals. Should there be selective breeding among humans? Is monogamy unnatural?

These examples suggest that there is no easy way to establish the 'final cause' that will enable us to say with certainty that we know exactly what every thing or action is for, or what part it has to play in an overall purposeful scheme of the universe.

The idea that the universe as a whole has a purpose and direction, and that it (and everything in it) has been created for a specific reason, is not a matter for scientific examination, but for religious belief. Those without such belief will not necessarily see a rationally justified 'final cause'. Indeed, one of the main arguments against belief in God has been the apparent pointlessness of suffering. Once pointlessness replaces purpose as a general view of the natural world, then the 'natural law' argument starts to break down.

Moral statements cannot be established by the observation of facts; you cannot argue from what 'is' to what 'ought to be' the case.

When you record facts, you do just that; facts are neutral in terms of ethics. Once you make a moral statement, however, you bring in values and wishes, you recommend that something should be done, or you express feelings. These things are over and above the facts to which they are applied.

At first sight, the 'natural law' argument seems to argue from something that 'is' (the nature of the world) to what 'ought' to be done. It does this on the basis of belief in a creator God who guarantees that things have a purpose which suits their nature, and to which they can freely respond in a positive and creative way.

A situation

Two adults of the same sex are attracted to one another. They wish to express that attraction physically, to live together with the same legal and social support that they would receive as a heterosexual couple, to adopt children, and to bring them up in a family home. Is what they wish to do morally right?

* Until the 1967 Sexual Offences Act, homosexual acts between consenting male adults were regarded as crimes in Britain. They were then made legal for those who had reached the age of 21 (as opposed to heterosexual acts, which are legal from the age of 16). In some Muslim countries, following strict Shari'ah laws, homosexuality is punishable by death. By contrast, in Classical Greece, homosexual love was widely practised, and socially acceptable. There is therefore no universally held view about homosexuality and its place in society.
* Since homosexuality involves what used to be called 'unnatural acts', it is a particularly suitable situation against which to test 'natural law' as an ethical theory.

This is how a 'natural law' argument might view that homosexual partnership:

* According to natural law, the purpose of sex is procreation. Since homosexual acts cannot lead to conception, they are 'unnatural' and therefore wrong.
* On this basis, heterosexual acts within a stable relationship (i.e. one that will enable children to be nurtured) or celibacy are the only morally acceptable sexual choices.

* Because of this, there is no moral objection, according to natural law principles, to the couple living together, or feeling attracted towards one another. The only objection is to any physical sexual acts that may take place between them.
* Because they cannot form a 'natural' family group, a natural law argument would suggest that homosexual couples should not be allowed to adopt children, who 'naturally' thrive only with the benefit of both mother and father role models.

Against this line of argument:

* One might argue that the presence of sexual organs in a human being implies that he or she is designed for sexual activity and the conception of children – in which case, celibacy is as unnatural as homosexuality, since it is a denial of the complete natural function of procreation. If this is established, then it is illogical to accept a celibate partnership between those who are sexually attracted.
* Some people are naturally attracted by members of the same sex. They experience their feelings as completely natural. Any difficulties that arise are the result of social conditioning, not nature.
* Sexuality can be said to achieve three ends:
  1 physical pleasure
  2 the deepening of a relationship
  3 the conception of children
* Only the third end is precluded by homosexual relationships. But is not the search for pleasure and for deep relationships as natural as the conception of children? If a marriage is known to be infertile, are heterosexual acts between its partners therefore immoral simply because conception is impossible?
* Marriage is a social function, and promiscuity can be practised equally by homosexuals and heterosexuals. The fact that homosexual couples cannot marry does not preclude deep and permanent relationships.

* If a homosexual couple form a stable relationship, they may be able to offer children a home that is, at the very least, as valuable to their upbringing as one in which there is either a single parent, or a heterosexual couple with a bad relationship. Hence, it would seem illogical to discriminate in this matter.

The introduction of civil partnerships in the UK, in December 2005, was recognition that stable homosexual relationships deserved the same legal and financial protection enjoyed by heterosexual couples who marry.

In pointing out some of the ways in which the 'natural law' view of the homosexual couple's situation might be challenged, it is not intended to undermine the principle of natural law as such, but to show that there are some areas of morality – particularly where relationships are concerned – where it is difficult to consider morality mainly in terms of specific actions.

Insight

Although in this section we focus on Aristotle's contribution to the 'natural law' approach to ethics, there is another important aspect to his ethics: paying attention. The virtuous person is one who pays thoughtful attention to everything that he or she does, acting thoughtfully. Thought attention to food, for example, will avoid either starvation or gluttony, but will tend to eat moderately – an example of Aristotle's famous 'mean' between extremes. That's an essential part of the ethical life; simply to pay attention to what we are doing and why we are doing it.

Are we naturally good or bad?

The philosopher Thomas Hobbes (1588–1679), in his book *Leviathan*, saw the life of man in a natural state as 'solitary, poor, nasty, brutish and short'. He took the view that, left to their own devices, people are naturally greedy. They want freedom, but also power (which included riches, reputation, success, nobility and eloquence – all that might give one person an advantage over others), and the inevitable result of this is that they would struggle against one another in order to gain it. In such a society, everyone is judged by his or her power:

> **The value, or WORTH of a man, is as of all other things, his price; that is to say, so much as would be given for the use of his power: and therefore is not absolute, but a thing dependent on the need and judgement of another.**

Unbridled competition, allied to seeing everyone in terms of his or her power, may lead to social anarchy. Hobbes therefore argued that it was in the self-interest of all, for people to set aside their claim to total power in order that they might live peacefully with others, for otherwise there will be constant danger of losing everything. In effect, he came down to a form of the 'golden rule' – do as you would be done to. He applied reason to human society, pointing out what was needed for society to function – but recognized that, without reason, people would be in a state of self-destructive greed and anarchy.

Such anarchy would not have been tolerated for long by Niccolo Machiavelli (1469–1527), who (in *The Prince*) argues that a ruler must know how to use his power and needs to be feared as well as respected by his people. His views on political power, and the measures that a person should be prepared to employ in order to gain and maintain it, suggest that in a natural state, humankind is ruthless and competitive. Both Hobbes and Machiavelli see natural life as essentially a struggle for power and survival.

By contrast, Jean-Jacques Rousseau (1712–78) thought that people were born essentially good – as was everything that came directly from nature. He argued that, if the conditions are right, people will flourish and be morally good. Human nature is fine in itself; the trouble is with the way in which society is organized. If temptation is put in people's way, a certain number of them are going to fall for it. This way of thinking led many twentieth-century socialists to assume that, once the dictatorship of the proletariat arrived, a just society would be established and all would be well. It also finds expression in the caricature of the social worker who, defending a criminal, lays all the blame on the circumstances of his or her upbringing, thereby diminishing moral responsibility.

Another example of this positive attitude to the natural is Henry David Thoreau (1817–62). In *Walden*, or *Life in the Woods*, he saw God within all nature and everything as therefore inherently good. He argued that people spent too much time worrying about earning a living, and seeking for things they do not really need – leading lives of 'quiet desperation'. By contrast, he sought a far simpler and more natural way of living.

For now we need only recognize that human life is complex, and that it is seldom possible to see what it would be like without the constraints of society. Opinion is divided:

* Are human beings fundamentally ruthless and savage, restrained and tamed by society, but liable at times to revert to their 'natural' behaviour?
* Or are human beings fundamentally good and caring, made antisocial and brutalized by society, but, given the right environment, capable of reverting to their gentler nature?

Points for reflection

* Looking at items in any newspaper, consider whether you believe humankind to be more 'Hobbes' or more 'Rousseau' (to use an extreme form: more 'savages tamed by society' or more 'angels corrupted by society').
* What do these views suggest about punishment and reform?
* Should society have more rules or fewer?
* Should morality be left to the conscience of the individual, or imposed by society?
* Aristotle saw reason as the distinctive human quality. Was he right?
* John Stuart Mill pointed out that most of the things people are punished for doing (e.g. murder, rape) are common occurrences in nature. Should ethics be seen therefore as a distinctively human step away from the natural order?
* Watch a cat 'play' with a mouse.

4

looking for
results

It is generally agreed that, in acting morally, people seek to achieve some benefit, either for themselves or others. It would therefore seem reasonable to judge actions right or wrong in terms of the benefits achieved: it is wrong to cause harm, right to give happiness or alleviate suffering.

There is a long tradition of ethical thinking that seeks to make overall benefit or happiness the goal of the ethical life – including, particularly, the Epicureans in Ancient Greece – but we shall focus in this chapter on the most influential of such approaches, and probably the most popular and widely accepted of all moral arguments: utilitarianism.

In general, utilitarianism claims that the right thing to do in any given situation is that which is likely to produce the greatest happiness (or benefit) to the greatest number of people involved. Developed by Jeremy Bentham and J.S. Mill, it is central to the work of probably the best-known ethical thinker today, Peter Singer.

Jeremy Bentham (1748–1832) argued for the **Principle of Utility**, by which he meant that an action should be judged according to the results it achieved. This approach to ethics is called **utilitarianism**. It has been one of the most influential of ethical theories, and the one most widely used in ordinary 'common sense' decisions.

Bentham argued that an action should be judged according to its ability to offer happiness or benefit to everyone involved, or to avoid unhappiness and pain. He thought that all should be treated equally, and did not consider one form of happiness to be more important than another, although he took such things as the intensity and duration of happiness into account.

In his book *Utilitarianism*, John Stuart Mill (1806–73) further developed this theory, allowing that the effect of rules should also be taken into account, where their observance would benefit society as a whole. He also denied that all forms of happiness were of equal status, distinguishing higher (e.g. intellectual or cultural) and lower (e.g. sensual) pleasures.

In its simplest form, utilitarianism states that, in any situation where there is a moral choice, **the right thing to do is that which is likely to produce the greatest happiness for the greatest number of people** – a formula that had been proposed in 1725 by Francis Hutcheson (1694–1746) as a way of assessing political regimes, the best nation being that which produced the most happiness, or benefit, for the most people.

This seems a very straightforward approach to ethical decisions. But it raises two important points:

1 **How do you evaluate the results of an action?**
   * Is happiness or benefit to be judged entirely by the individuals concerned, or is there some more objective way of assessing it?
   * In other words, what are your criteria for saying that a result is 'good'?

In December 2009, there was a debate in the UK about whether there should be minimum price for a unit of alcohol, in an attempt to discourage the growth in consumption and consequent increase in alcohol-related illness and death. Against this, it was argued that it is wrong to punish a responsible majority because of the foolishness of a minority. Some blamed the extension of licensing hours, others criticized supermarkets for offering cheap drink. But supermarkets work in a competitive environment, and the increase in licensing hours was intended to bring about more civilized drinking and avoid a rush before 'closing time'.

In these and many other situations, action is taken on the basis of a predicted result which may prove to be quite false. Longer opening hours or an increase in the cost of alcohol may or may not change drinking habits. You may fix one problem only to create another, or offer benefits to some at the cost of harming others.

The aim may indeed be to produce the greatest benefit for the greatest number, but there can be many different routes to that end, and deciding between them may not be easy.

2 What if the results of an action are ambiguous?

* How do you balance the unhappiness caused to one person against the happiness of many?
* Is immediate happiness the criterion, or is it the longer-term benefit?

For example, some would recommend that young offenders should be given a prison sentence, in the hope that it would encourage them to reform and thus not re-offend. This could imply that – although it is not experienced as such – the punishment may be regarded as increasing the happiness of the offender in the long term, as well as offering added happiness to those in society that he or she will not offend against in the future.

* By what criteria do you judge what leads to happiness in this case? If you act against someone's wishes, claiming

that it is 'really' for their greater happiness, you presumably do so on the basis of your idea of what constitutes the good life. On what is that idea based?

The smiling headmaster of old who brandished a cane saying 'It's for your own good!' may have believed just that. But could it be proved? More and more evidence could be brought, and yet there would never be certainty. Some would point to occasions of genuine reform, others to establishing a cult of brutality.

Forms of utilitarianism

Act utilitarianism

Act utilitarianism looks for the results of an individual act in order to assess whether that act is right or wrong. In this form, utilitarianism accepts no general rules except the rule that one should seek the greatest happiness (or benefit – remember this is not a matter of emotions but of welfare) of the greatest number.

Act utilitarianism requires an assessment about pain or happiness that is related to each individual action. But the perceived results of an action may be explicable only in terms of social convention, not in terms of actual pain inflicted. People may choose to suffer – it is their happiness – but this may not be perceived by the external observer.

Example

You observe a scene of extreme suffering. A crowd of people hobbling, shuffling and obviously in pain run between lines of onlookers. You observe their exhaustion, and learn that they have run 26 miles and, in doing so, have suffered blisters, cramp and other aches and pains. Suppose you see one of them, at the limit of his or her endurance, slow to a walking pace, but the crowd of onlookers shouts that he or she should continue running.

Such action could be regarded as cruelty on a mass scale, yet thousands of people the world over will choose to go through just such an ordeal, pushing themselves to the limit. Voluntary suffering may be idiotic, but it is not immoral unless, by accepting it, genuine harm is done to others. A person who is determined to run a marathon in spite of medical warnings to the contrary, risks his or her life and all the suffering that their death could cause their family, so that might be regarded as immoral. Otherwise, running a marathon is an example of the acceptance of pain for no obvious result (other than that of personal satisfaction).

Pleasure and pain are therefore to be set in a social context, and may be misunderstood. It might be possible, for example, by arguing that it inspires others to get fit, to justify a marathon in strictly utilitarian terms, but it is by no means the straightforward assessment of pain or pleasure that act utilitarianism assumes.

Rule utilitarianism

This rather more sophisticated approach to utilitarianism was put forward by John Stuart Mill, as follows.

* Intellectual pleasures should be preferred to immediate physical pleasures, and one should assess the quality of the pleasure anticipated as well as the quantity.
  (In this he followed the Epicurean tradition.)
* People may sacrifice themselves (e.g. losing their life in the attempt to save others), but that such sacrifice is not of value in itself, only in terms of what it achieves.

He took an important step in allowing a utilitarian assessment to take into account those rules that benefit society as a whole. So, for example, the rule that it is wrong to take innocent human life is of general benefit to society, and should therefore not be broken, even if, in a particular case, killing an innocent person might seem to benefit other people. Thus the utilitarian can use general rules and principles, on the grounds that those principles have themselves been framed on utilitarian grounds.

As it has developed, those who take this line of argument have divided between:

* strong rule utilitarians, who hold that one should not break one of these general rules to fit individual situations, and

* weak rule utilitarians, who would allow the pleasure or pain involved in a particular situation to take precedence over the general rule, while still allowing the general rule and its benefits to be taken into consideration.

Fluoride in water

Fluoride, a substance found naturally in water supplies in some places, is good for teeth. Hence it would seem that a utilitarian argument should be in favour of introducing fluoride into water everywhere, so that all may benefit.

However, it can also be argued that people should be free to decide whether or not they accept treatment, and that it is generally wrong to impose a remedy, even if it is known to be of benefit. A strong rule utilitarian argument might therefore oppose the universal introduction of fluoride (on the grounds that it would go against the beneficial rule that people should be free to choose) whereas a weak rule utilitarian argument would try to achieve a balance between known benefits and the modest loss of personal freedom of choice.

Preference utilitarianism

Preference utilitariarism says that you should take into account the preferences of the person concerned in each case, unless those preferences are outweighed by the preferences of other people. In other words, this form allows people to say what for them constitutes pleasure or pain. It does not allow one person to impose his or her own criterion of pleasure on others, nor to make a utilitarian assessment on that basis.

Preference utilitarianism has become probably the most widely used ethical theory in areas of applied and professional ethics, largely due to the work of Peter Singer, whose books (especially *Practical Ethics*, published in 1979) have been immensely influential. Singer's work has been widely criticized by those seeking a traditional and absolutist approach. His basic principle is that one should seek an 'equal consideration of interests'. That does not mean that all have equal rights or should be treated equally, but that each should be treated in a way that is appropriate. Consideration will be given to the interests of animals, for example, but not by treating them as though they were people. Equally, someone who has been brain damaged and is in a persistent vegetative state does not have interests identical to those of someone who is conscious.

Peter Singer's work on ethics goes far beyond a simply case for preference utilitarianism. He argues, for example, that there are two things that make life worthwhile: the reduction in the amount of pain in the universe; and commitment to a cause that is beyond oneself. These, which provide a starting point for the ethical life, bring a sense of fulfilment and meaning. In other words, life becomes meaningful if you try to make the world a better place. Singer's work in ethics is challenging, in that it goes beyond simple utilitarianism, and touches the fundamental question about what it means to live an ethical life.

Starting with the situation ...

Utilitarianism works in a way that is the opposite to that of natural law: natural law starts with theories about the nature of the world and the purpose in life. From those general theories, it looks at each and every action and object and asks about its purpose. Once that is known, it claims that the right thing to do is that which fulfils the natural purpose, and the wrong thing is that which frustrates it. You start from principles, and apply them to individual situations.

With utilitarianism, the opposite is the case. You start with the pain or pleasure involved in individual situations and then take into account the wider pain or pleasure involved by the application of general rules, or the preferences of the people involved. The starting point, however, is with the immediate situation.

What the two approaches have in common is their desire to find some external, objective criterion (whether the pleasure or pain involved, or the purpose to be fulfilled) by which to show that an action is right or wrong.

In theory, using either of these approaches, it should be possible to present a case for morality which is convincing to other people, for it can be set out and demonstrated.

The limitation of the utilitarian approach, as we have seen, is that there is never enough evidence to provide certainty. It is always possible that the future will not turn out as we expect, and that our intention to maximize benefit will actually increase harm.

General criticisms of utilitarianism

Society is complex. It does not consist of uniform people, all wanting the same things or expressing the same preferences. There will always be conflict of interests, divergence of views. Utilitarianism has taken this into account to a certain extent by allowing for 'preferences' to be expressed, rather than imposing on others what we consider to be for their greatest happiness. Nevertheless, the final decision is made in the interests of the majority, thus making it difficult to justify action on behalf of an individual or minority group. Any sense of social justice seems to demand that there should be cases where the majority freely give up something to their benefit for the sake of a minority or an individual.

Example

Sometimes, as a result of an appeal on television, the attention of a whole nation is focused on the plight of an individual. This is made especially poignant if the individual is a child desperate for a life-saving operation, or a local hero who is injured in the course of helping others. In these circumstances, offers of help are given that are out of all proportion to what would be allocated on a strictly utilitarian assessment of need.

* Are these the result of emotional indulgence rather than rational assessment of need?
* If so, is it wrong to give help to an individual in these circumstances?

A narrowly utilitarian assessment may preclude action being taken on behalf of an individual, on the grounds that it is not in the interests of the majority that so much relief should be expended on a single person. On the other hand, if the majority are presented with the facts in a way that engages them emotionally, they may well freely give up something (generally money, offered to the needy cause) in order that the individual may benefit. In this case, although the end result is an unequal sharing of resources, the preference of a majority of those involved – that they wish to give money – is satisfied. On strictly utilitarian terms, it would be wrong only if the preferences of the donors were outweighed by the preferences of those opposed to the donations being given. As always, the utilitarian assessment remains inconclusive.

Utilitarianism deflects our attention from the personal convictions and values that lie at the heart of moral choices, and makes the decision one that requires external assessment and calculation. But moral responses are not always a matter of conforming to what is reasonable, but of following convictions about what is 'right' even if it does not obviously lead to an increase in happiness.

Often, when a moral choice has to be made, there is no time to calculate who will benefit and by how much. One has to act without knowing all the consequences. In such situations, my choice of action, often spontaneous, is based on convictions, not calculations.

A situation

A mother, walking along a river bank, hears a shout from behind her and turns to see her child topple off a bicycle into the raging torrent. She plunges into the water, but is swept to her death, along with her child.

A utilitarian, confronted with information about the woman's remaining five, now motherless, children, and her work as a doctor, saving the lives of many, might say that she should not, on balance, have plunged into the water.

But is it possible, in all honesty, to say that she was not acting morally in attempting that hopeless rescue? And who, listening to the oration at such a person's funeral, would not wish, if put to a similar test, to have similar courage?

I am not arguing that a person who did not attempt the rescue could not perfectly well have justified his or her decision to stand by and watch the child drown. Indeed, it might take great courage to do that. But is it the only morally correct option?

Perhaps a situation that illustrates this in its starkest form is given in William Styron's novel *Sophie's Choice*. It explores the guilt of a woman, living in the USA, who had survived a Nazi concentration camp. Gradually the source of her terrible sense of guilt is revealed: she was held in the camp with her two children and was told that one could be saved but the other would be sent to die. But she must choose which: if not, both would die. She made the choice – knowing that, by doing so, she has condemned the other. She is haunted by that choice.

* From a utilitarian point of view, she did the right thing. To have refused to make a choice would have made it certain that both children would die.
* Equally, she is not to blame, because she did not actually choose that either child should die – she was not directly the agent of their deaths.
* But is it possible to live with such a choice? Does a utilitarian justification make the decision any more bearable?

There would seem to be two major limitations to the utilitarian standpoint:

1 Utilitarianism, because it focuses on results, which are external to the person making the moral choice, does not adequately take into account the motive for making a choice – and yet it is motivation which would seem to be important in the assessment of whether a person was behaving in a moral way.

2 Utilitarianism does not explain why people sometimes feel that there are moral rules that should not be broken, irrespective of the consequences. This is a feature of moral dilemmas, and it is one to which we shall turn in the next chapter.

There is one final thing to be said about utilitarianism. It is a popular approach, which appears to offer clear-cut ways of assessing what is right. The problem is that life is seldom so straightforward. Few would argue that utilitarianism is not a valuable rule of thumb for assessing what a reasonable person might choose to do. The question is whether (taken in isolation from all the other reasons why people choose to do one thing rather than another) it is adequate as an ethical theory. Human motivation is subtle, and people may justify their actions by reference to ideology, religion, ambition, personal need and so on. It is seldom simply a matter of weighing up the likely results and then making a choice – although such assessment may be a useful tool for a subsequent justification of a choice made instinctively, or from confused motivation.

5

the experience of moral choice

Whereas the Natural Law and Utilitarian approaches to ethics sought to ground morality objectively, either in a sense of natural purpose or in anticipated results, Immanuel Kant – a hugely influential eighteenth-century philosopher – took as his starting point the experience of a sense of duty and an unconditional moral 'ought'.

In what is described as his 'categorical imperative' he sets out three very general, rational bases for testing out moral claims: that one should be prepared for everyone to act on the same moral principle as oneself; that people should be treated as ends rather than means; that one should act as thought legislating for a situation where everyone is treated as a free and autonomous individual.

He also argued that, even if our actions are predictable from an objective, scientific point of view, we still experience ourselves as free agents, and therefore both experience the moral 'ought' and are required to accept moral responsibility.

Whether through conscience or through thinking about right and wrong, the experience of moral choice comes in the form of a sense that there is something I 'ought' to do regardless of the consequences. This is sometimes called a **categorical imperative**. Notice this distinction:

* A *hypothetical imperative* takes the form 'If you want to achieve X then do Y.'
* A *categorical imperative* takes the form 'You should do Y.' It is absolute, having no conditions attached to it.

The thinker most associated with this 'categorical imperative' is Immanuel Kant (1724–1804). Being an eighteenth-century German Protestant, he was very much concerned with the sense of duty. You do your duty (what you understand to be right) without regard to consequences. His main work on this is *Groundwork of the Metaphysics of Morals* (1785).

Kant held that the categories we use to understand the world – categories like space, time and causality – are not to be found in the data of our experience but are imposed on our experience by our own minds. We cannot prove that everything has a cause, but our minds automatically look for causes. **The mind plays an active part in shaping and ordering experience; it is not merely a passive recipient of what is 'out there'.** This is sometimes referred to as Kant's 'Copernican Revolution': just as Copernicus showed that the Earth revolved round the Sun, and not vice versa, so Kant showed that our minds determine the way in which we experience things.

In the same way, Kant argued that we would never be able to show conclusively that a certain action was right or wrong by reference to its expected results, because we would never have enough evidence, and might disagree about how to interpret it. The starting point for morals cannot therefore be something 'out there' among the data interpreted by our senses, but should be the actual experience of moral obligation – the feeling that there is something we 'ought' to do.

> In other words, you do not first find out what is 'right' and then feel that you ought to do it; rather, that which you feel you ought to do is what you mean by 'right'.

Kant argued that to do your duty you have to exclude two other considerations: effects (or results) and inclinations. If you decide to do something, expecting that you will benefit by it, that is not a moral choice. Equally, if you decide to do something because you enjoy doing it, that is not a moral choice either. Kant also rejected external moral authority where it conflicted with personal moral conviction. Unthinking obedience is not a valid moral position – **one should act out of a personal sense of what is right**. His starting point is the 'good will', aided by the pure practical reason.

Kant therefore sought to set out in the general principles of morality, the absolute and rational requirements of the *categorical imperative* (the unconditioned 'ought'), which might be applied to all moral issues. What is more, he sought to do this 'a priori' – based on reason alone, not on the evidence about how people actually behave or the results of their actions. There are three main forms of his categorical imperative:

1 Act only on that maxim (or principle) which you can, at the same time, wish to make a universal law.
2 Act in such a way as to treat people as ends and never as means.
3 Act as though a legislating member of the kingdom of ends.

The implication of the first, and major, form is that I should only do something if I am prepared for everyone else to be free to act according to that same moral principle. This does not mean that I can only do something if I imagine everyone else doing it as well (that might well cause practical chaos), but I must be prepared for everyone else to follow the same logical principle. I should not consider myself to be a unique or special case.

Notice what this does not tell you. It does not tell you what the content of your moral decision should be; it does not say that this or that action is always right or wrong. Rather it provides a general principle – our willingness to see the basis of our action become a universal law.

There is a general question to ask of a theory such as Kant's: is it possible to give a general rule that can be applied to each and every particular act, or is it essential to know the particular purpose and context of that act, before deciding on its moral status?

Example

Breaking a promise

Is it ever morally right to make a promise knowing that one has no intention of keeping it? If I consider, at the moment when I make a promise, that I shall be free to break it, then – according to Kant's first form of the categorical imperative – I should be willing everyone else to be free to make and break their promises. But Kant argues that this would make nonsense of the whole idea of making a promise, and it is therefore illogical to say that it is right to make a promise that one does not intend to keep.

The second form of the categorical imperative follows from the first. If you are prepared to universalize the principles on which you act, it implies that you are prepared to consider everyone else as an autonomous moral agent, also free to act on their freely chosen maxims. And that, of course, implies that they should be treated as ends in themselves, never as means to your own end. This aspect of Kant meets with almost universal approval. Most people would see any treatment of people as though they were 'things', disposable or merely there for our own personal convenience, as fundamentally wrong. Relationships in which one person exploits another are generally regarded as morally wrong, whatever the particular circumstances.

Insight

Recognition of the right of each person to be treated as a full, autonomous human agent is fundamental to Kant, but is also implied by the other ethical arguments considered in this book.

The third form follows from the second. Kant argues that you should always imagine yourself as being in the position of someone who is responsible for legislating for a society in which everyone is to be treated as an 'end', an autonomous individual. What is the right thing to do in such a society?

Notice that Kant sees the important touchstones as rationality (can you justify it in a rational way?) and universality (can you apply it to everyone?). The implication of this is that each individual constructs, and takes responsibility for, his or her own set of moral values, based on **duty** and the **good will**.

This is very different from the natural law or utilitarian approaches, and sometimes their priorities conflict, as in the following situation.

The cost of truth

You are held by a terrorist gang, who demand to know the whereabouts of a close friend or relative whom they clearly wish to kill. You know that the person concerned is in hiding. Do you tell the truth and admit that you know where they are, or do you tell a lie, either by giving the wrong location, or by saying that you do not know where they are?

Here the dilemma is between anticipating the harm that will be done if you tell the truth and your friend is killed, and the general moral principle that you should tell the truth.

You might want to argue that anyone, confronted similarly by the prospect of the death of an innocent person, should lie. In this case, although the rule about telling the truth could be universalized, so also could the rule about doing anything necessary in order to prevent innocent suffering.

The dilemma is caused by a clash between a utilitarian assessment (that telling the truth will end up causing suffering) and obeying a general principle of truth telling, established rationally.

Kant also suggested that, if you respond to an unconditional moral 'ought', doing so presupposes three things, which he termed the postulates of the pure practical reason:

* **God** – because there must be a sense that, by doing one's duty, happiness will follow, and that is something that could only be possible in a world ordered by God.
* **Freedom** – because, unless you experience yourself as free, you will have no sense of being able to make a moral choice.
* **Immortality** – because you know that you might not see the results of all that you do in this life, and therefore presuppose that there is some future in which the present imbalance of actions and rewards will be rectified.

Kant does not mean that you have to believe in these three things in order to respond to an 'ought' but that, once you do acknowledge the unconditional nature of that 'ought', it implies that you believe in them.

Not everyone would accept this, for it is based on the idea that there is a rational structure to our thought that underlies our instinctive reactions. This may not be so. We may feel an obligation for the worst of motives, or from unconscious needs.

This highlights a major problem with Kant's ethics. It is designed for a world where people act out of good will and moral duty. In the real world people are far more complex, seldom completely rational in their moral and personal choices, and sometimes act out of plain hatred or ill will. Is it wise, in such a world, to remain a moral innocent?

Determined and yet free?

Kant argued that our minds impose space, time and causality on the phenomena that they encounter. From an external point of view, everything is conditioned. When I observe someone else making a choice, my mind naturally seeks out the causes that led to that particular choice. In the world of phenomena, there can be no freedom. But Kant held that all we know about are the phenomena that come through our senses. We know things as they appear to us, not things as they are in themselves. (Things-in-themselves Kant calls **noumena**, our perception of them **phenomena**.)

On this basis, Kant is able to say that we are *at one and the same time* phenomenally conditioned (perceived from the outside, I have no freedom), and noumenally free (I experience my freedom to act – something that I know, but nobody else can observe). There are therefore two ways of understanding the moral act:

* from the standpoint of one who observes the choices that are made, with their consequences and the implications they have for an understanding of humankind
* from the standpoint of the person who is actually confronted with a choice and who, in a moment of creative action, actually responds on the basis of his or her values and convictions.

This distinction is of crucial importance for ethics. When the logical positivists argued that the meaning of a statement was its method of verification, they dismissed ethics as meaningless, because it could not be verified by experience, in other words, by *phenomena*. And yet – as we saw in the reaction against that position – people continue to find moral statements meaningful. This highlights the division of perspective between a person who observes and analyses the phenomenon of human activity, and what it is to experience a moral 'ought'. As we are in ourselves, we can act morally, and no amount of analysis and observation is going to be able to remove either the experience of freedom and choice, or its moral significance.

6

personal development and virtue

Before the sixteenth century, moral thinking was dominated by Aristotle's idea of Natural Law (as interpreted through Christian theologians) and the authority of religion. With the Reformation and the intellectual upheavals that followed, this was replaced by attempts to find a rational basis for morality, of which we have looked at utilitarianism and Kantian ethics.

But instead of seeking a rational or objective basis for morality, can we simply create our own values? Can we stop asking what *is* right and start deciding what *will be* right? In this chapter we look at Nietzsche's attempt to do just that.

We shall do so in the context of asking whether it is possible or right to make our own personal development a basis for ethics, whether people are inherently selfish or whether they can be genuinely altruistic, and what it means to seek human flourishing by cultivating the virtues.

Altruism?

Can human beings act genuinely for the benefit of others?

Thomas Hobbes, in *Leviathan* (1651), argued that, if people voluntarily give up their rights for the benefit of others, they do so in order to achieve something good for themselves. Indeed, he claimed that every voluntary act had as its aim some good to be obtained for the person performing it. On this basis, although the benefit done to oneself may be less tangible than the benefit offered to the other person (e.g. feeling good for having been charitable), nevertheless in some way, even if we appear to be helping others, we are actually acting in a way that benefits ourselves.

By contrast, Hume's *Enquiry Concerning the Principles of Morals* (1751) takes the view that people do actually experience 'sympathy' – that is, they respond when they see the suffering or the joy of others. He makes this experience basic to his ethics, in that if there were no sympathy there would be no development of altruistic qualities.

This does not mean that people respond to the sufferings of others in a generous way all the time, rather that everyone can experience some degree of sympathy. A psychopath, for example, is someone who has no sense of right or wrong, and who is not going to be persuaded by reason, but who has urges (to kill, for example) that are totally devoid of any sense of sympathy for his or her victim. In other words, for the psychopath, other people are 'things', not fellow human beings who have feelings and to whom one might want to relate in a personal way. In this case, the exception illustrates the general rule – that people are capable of responding to the sufferings of others.

Hume also holds that people can exhibit qualities that give happiness to themselves as well as being useful to others. These 'virtues' include justice, faithfulness and politeness, which are not directly related to self-development or happiness, but to the interests of others. In fact, Hume regards *benevolence* as the highest quality of which human nature is capable.

In section 9 of the *Enquiry* ... Hume seems to step back from saying that sympathy is always its own justification. He points out that, even if someone appears to lose out personally because of some action for the benefit of others, he or she will feel inner peace of mind and satisfaction – which lead to personal happiness.

Notice that Hume is not saying that one should show sympathy *because* it leads to peace of mind, but that peace of mind happens to be a result of the genuine response of sympathy (unlike Hobbes, who seems to be saying that sympathy is merely disguised self-love).

So, in assessing personal development as a feature of morality we need to reflect on three possibilities:

* That people are basically selfish, and if they are honest they will admit it.
* That people think they are unselfish and considerate to others but, in fact, they are really just satisfying their own deeper needs.
* That people can genuinely feel and respond to the situations of others, and can show honest altruism.

There is one other important feature of Hume's idea of 'sympathy' to keep in mind. When we looked at Aristotle in Chapter 3, we saw that he attempted to get some objective criterion for moral statements. His idea of what was right stemmed from reason, and an intellectual conception about the purpose of human existence. Hume, by contrast, sees reason as taking a secondary role to the emotions. It is the latter that provide us with the values we need for directing our action; reason is their handmaid, selecting options and possibilities to enable them to be expressed in practical action.

If a person is to develop, that development takes place within a social context. In other words, personal development implies personal worth in terms of relationships. It would be difficult to develop personally in total isolation from others, and if a person could achieve a high degree of personal growth in isolation (for example, through some form of religious asceticism), it would still depend on the religious and social ideas that set up the conditions for that growth in the first place. This social context was emphasized by F.H. Bradley in an essay called 'My station and its duties' (in *Ethical Studies*, 1876). Bradley argued that self-realization was the basis of ethics, and he followed the philosopher Hegel in pointing out that people need both self-expression and recognition if they are to enjoy the good life. That recognition can come through family relationships, through local society or through the state, because (according to Hegel) these are the basic spheres of influence.

Central to Bradley (and Hegel) is the idea that self-realization (achieving one's full potential as a unique human being) takes place in society, not in isolation. If freedom is needed to allow for the personal development and autonomy of an individual, we need to remember that it comes with a price, and that one person's freedom may well curtail that of another.

Nietzsche

The thinker who most radically challenged traditional moral thinking and placed human development at the centre of a value creating system of thought was Friedrich Nietzsche.

It is often valuable to consider a thinker's work against the background of his or her personal circumstances – although with many philosophers this is discouraged by the way that they present ideas in a cogent fashion, inviting logical comment only. Nietzsche is different. His writing is vivid, and his ideas are sometimes presented as images. It may be worth reflecting therefore that he was born in 1844, the son of a Lutheran pastor and of the daughter of a country vicar, and that as a young man he was a lover of solitude, enthusiastically religious, and also highly talented.

We shall approach Nietzsche's work through four key features.

'God is dead'

The first of these is the idea that **God is dead**. This is not a casual comment from one who has not taken religious seriously; it is a conclusion about the state of things as Nietzsche saw them in the 1880s. In *The Joyous Science* he has the image of a madman who comes into the town with the message that 'God is dead': not that God had never existed, but that people had killed him. The character asks if his hearers do not sense that it is growing darker, that they need lamps, even at noon. He tries to explain that people have cut the world loose, and that (without God) it is wandering without fixed values and without direction.

This is perhaps the starkest recognition of what had taken place, almost since the Reformation – the replacement of an authoritarian and metaphysical structure of thought, believed to have been given by God, by human reason. His point was that, whatever they may claim to believe, people in fact create values based on themselves, not on God. They are the centre and measure of life. Without God, humankind is forced to take responsibility and establish its own values.

'Superman'

The next feature is the **superman** (a rather poor translation of *Übermensch*, which means something that goes over or beyond man). In *Thus Spoke Zarathustra*, the sage Zarathustra comes down his mountain. He opens his teaching by saying:

> *I teach you the Superman. Man is something that should be overcome. What have you done to overcome him? All creatures hitherto have created something beyond themselves: and do you want to be the ebb of this great tide, and return to the animals rather than overcoming man?*

(translated by Hollingdale, Penguin, p. 41)

Here the context is evolution. As the ape is to humans, so humans will be to the superman. He then takes an important step: 'The Superman is the meaning of the earth. Let your will say: The Superman *shall* be the meaning of the earth!' In other words, from this moment on humanity is to choose its values and its direction by an act of will. We humans are to be the creators of value. Nietzsche is critical of those who sought some heavenly goal, accusing them of being poisoners, weakening humankind. Instead, the true goal is to be found in the future – the *Übermensch*. It is an affirmation of life, and of the human will that shapes and determines that life. In other words, you are free to define your world!

'The will to power'

The third feature is the **will to power** – which is the force behind Nietzsche's moral thinking. It does not mean a crude attempt to get power, but the affirmation of life, and the will to develop and move forward. It is the will to power that, for Nietzsche, is the source of all values and therefore the source of morality.

Nietzsche's thought is highly individualistic. Wanting to be equal with others and showing humility – key features of democracy and Christianity, as he sees them – are signs of decadence and weakness. They sap the will to power and desire for personal development. For this reason, Nietzsche opposed both democracy and Christianity. According to Nietzsche, exploitation is one of the basic features of life, and self-development is fundamental. Therefore we should be free to adopt whatever means we need in order to secure that power. In *Beyond Good and Evil*, he sees the world as divided into masters and slaves, and he holds that the morality that suits the one will not suit the other. Masters are free to do what their own creative development requires. Nietzsche rejects both democracy and Christianity because they are associated with slave values, not with master values, and cause the decay of the state because they are based on the false assumption that all are equal. He also attacks Christianity because it allows people to deny themselves on Earth for the sake of God and a heavenly reward.

'The eternal recurrence'

Finally, there is the **eternal recurrence**. This is a difficult and complex idea. Perhaps it may be approached by contrasting it with the ideas of Aristotle or traditional Christian views. To Aristotle, everything has an end or a purpose. It achieves its goal once it fulfils that end. In the traditional Christian scheme, the world looks to something outside itself to justify its existence – God. But for Nietzsche, God is dead. There is no way that this present life can be simply tolerated because it leads to or points to something beyond itself.

Nietzsche therefore held that one should be prepared to accept life as it is; to affirm it and work with it.

His graphic way of presenting this is to pose the challenge of accepting that everything that happens will be repeated over and over again. Can you look at such an endlessly repeating life and still affirm it? Can you enjoy it just as it is, without asking for some external compensation or explanation? Nietzsche presents a challenge – a necessary challenge in any world that has consciously or unconsciously discarded religious belief and the old metaphysics that went with it. **The challenge of 'the eternal recurrence' is to accept life as it is.**

Nietzsche's writings *are* a challenge, and these notes hardly touch the surface of what he has to say on the topic of morality. They are included here because Nietzsche looks at morality in a way that is very different from the older 'natural law' and 'utilitarian' arguments – in place of a fixed purpose or happiness, the key to Nietzsche's morality is a commitment to the future of humankind.

A point for reflection

Through the 'will to power', one should 'give style' to one's character and the greatest enjoyment is 'to live dangerously!' In *Beyond Good and Evil*, Nietzsche said of morality: 'Every morality is a rationalization of fear, a set of safety instructions on how to live at peace with the most dangerous aspects of one's self.'

* What might a modern psychologist make of this?
* How is it possible to be afraid of aspects of oneself, or to regard oneself as dangerous?
* What might be the ethical implication of admitting that, consciously or unconsciously, we have a 'will to power' and that it is the source of our values?

Virtue ethics

Rather than starting with questions about whether a particular action is right or wrong, it is equally possible to approach ethics by asking what it means to be a 'good' person. In other words, we ask what virtues or qualities a person should possess if they are to live the good life.

This **virtue ethics** approach goes back to Aristotle, who was concerned to understand what constituted the good life. Virtues are those qualities that can enable someone to live well and fulfil themselves as a human being. There are various lists of virtues, but the **cardinal virtues** listed by the Ancient Greeks were temperance, justice, courage and prudence.

If these qualities enable a person to express and live out his or her true – or essential – nature, then there will be parallels between virtue ethics and the natural law approach that we examined in Chapter 3. Natural law understood morality in terms of conforming to one's essential nature; the virtues summarize the personal qualities that enable that to happen.

With the rise of utilitarianism and Kantian ethics, alongside the older Natural Law approach, the virtues had not featured much in ethical debates until the 1950s, when virtue ethics was examined again, particularly associated with the work of Phillipa Foot and Elizabeth Anscombe. Although the basic argument – seeing virtues as dispositions to act in a particular way, and as a means of self-fulfilment – was not new, what was new was that it shifted moral debate away from general rules and principles of behaviour and towards more general questions about value and meaning in life, and the qualities that were worth developing and encouraging.

In particular this appealed to feminist thinkers, who had seen the rationalism of other ethical theories as being influenced by particularly male ways of approaching life, based on rights and duties, whereas they sought a more 'feminine' approach that included a recognition of the value of relationships and intimacy.

It also had the advantage of being a naturalistic ethic, in that it moved away from the idea of simply obeying rules, to an appreciation of how one might express one's fundamental nature and thus fulfil one's potential as a human being. That had a great appeal to those who were critical of the narrowness of ethical debate, and who wanted to explore human potential in a much broader context.

There are important questions raised by virtue ethics:

* Do we have a fixed *essence*? Are there, for example, particular feminine qualities that all women should seek to express, and which constitute feminine virtues? Or is our nature dependent on our surroundings and upbringing?
* If there are different ways of expressing the same virtue (e.g. out of love, one person might seek euthanasia, another seek to prolong life), how should you choose between them? At that point, is it necessary to fall back on one of the other ethical theories?

Example

Consider the difference between murder, committed in the course of a robbery, and killing a loved one who is seriously ill, in order to prevent further suffering. The latter – euthanasia – is treated differently, because the intention of the person doing the killing is quite different. In the first example the vice displayed is greed, in the second, the virtue displayed is compassion, and that makes a fundamental difference to the moral significance of the act itself.

Notice here that moral praise of blame focuses on the virtues or vices of the people concerned, not on the absolute legality or results of their actions.

7

scepticism and relativism

So far we have been examining ethical theories that seek to establish a basis upon which one can make a rational decision about matters of right and wrong. But this whole enterprise may be challenged from two points of view: scepticism and relativism.

A sceptic – as the name implies – doubts our ability to establish a universal or general principle by which we can settle moral issues. Sometimes people take this view because the complex reality of life and the demands of particular situations do not seem compatible with any one clear, rational ethical system. We shall look at the political advice given by Machiavelli to illustrate this.

Equally, it is possible to argue that all moral norms are socially established, and therefore that different societies may have mutually incompatible sets of moral values between which that there is no rational way to decide whether any one is better than any other.

In the context of ethics, **scepticism** is the view that there are no solid foundations for ethical theories or principles. It may take the form of a scientific argument for a determinist position – thereby suggesting that freedom of choice is an illusion, and therefore that moral responsibility is also illusory. It may equally take the form of a logical argument that questions each assumption and attempts to show that there is no foundation for morality that cannot be challenged. It may even be expressed in the assumption that, whatever they may claim, people are only motivated by their own self-interest.

We shall look at one exponent of a political philosophy that comes as near as one might choose to scepticism, namely that of Machiavelli. Whether *The Prince* was taken to be serious advice for the aspiring ruler, or written with the wry smile of one who has long observed how people actually survive in the political jungle, need not greatly concern us. It does, however, offer a moral scepticism that verges on the cynical.

An equal threat to those who would espouse absolute moral principles is **relativism**. All ethical theories are relativist to some extent – in the sense that it is widely accepted that moral rules should be applied in a way that is sensitive to the particular situation and context. However, relativism can be pursued to the point of saying that all moral norms and principles originate within a social context. Hence they are not autonomous and cannot be applied universally. Society decides what is right or wrong, and may be free to change its mind.

Because relativism appears to be sensitive to the autonomy of the individual and the cultural context of human action, it tends to be more 'reasonable' and perhaps even more moral that scepticism. However, a thoroughgoing relativism makes moral debate very difficult, for debate depends on agreed principles and norms, and if these are culturally conditioned then they too can be challenged and dismissed.

Perhaps the question to ask in this chapter is whether the combined influence of scepticism and relativism invalidates the ethical arguments and theories that we have been considering so far, or whether they are simply a restraining influence on those who would define morality too narrowly.

Philosophers or politicians?

Kant was a professional philosopher, and by all accounts his life was regular and carefully ordered. His thought is precise and logical, as we saw in the examination of his 'categorical imperative' (see Chapter 5).

* He presents us with three simple rules – that we should be prepared to universalize the principles on which we act, that we should treat people as ends in themselves and not merely as means to our own ends, and we should act as though taking responsibility for legislating for a kingdom of ends. All three are eminently sensible criteria by which to assess our moral choices.
* He does not offer practical advice for specific situations, but the most general of guidelines.

Why then might one hesitate to accept Kant as the ultimate judge of acceptable action? Perhaps because in the actual world of crises and moral decisions, life is seldom as straightforward as it would seem from Kant's standpoint.

To get a realistic view of moral choices we need to balance what we feel 'ought' to happen by a study of what does actually happen. From Kant's perspective, much of what happens (especially, perhaps, in the world of politics) might be regarded as immoral. But is that fair? Should we not look carefully at the actual choices that people make if they are to rule? Should we not balance the innocent simplicity of the categorical imperative against the experience of one who sees the consequence of always acting innocently?

For a very different perspective we shall therefore turn to a politician – a fifteenth-century Italian from Florence, a diplomat and shrewd (if cynical) observer of the realities of political life. His maxims are rather different from those of Kant, and he treats morality with a good degree of scepticism!

Machiavelli

Machiavelli was essentially a practical man. His book *The Prince* gives advice to one who would seek to rule a principality, and it is set against the political intrigues of fifteenth- and sixteenth-century Italy. It looks at the realities of political life, the need for stern action, the need to use power in a way that is effective, the need to act creatively and decisively, breaking all the conventional moral rules if necessary in order to deal in a pragmatic way with the demands of high office.

Machiavelli's views are suitable to balance against Kant's for three reasons:

* Kant is concerned with the 'categorical imperative' – the 'ought' that does not depend on conditions. Machiavelli is concerned almost all the time with 'hypothetical imperatives', such as what you need to do in order to retain power. The implication of this is that, in most practical situations, it is the hypothetical rather than the categorical that constitutes the normal sphere of 'moral' (to Machiavelli) operations.

* Kant argues that you should always treat people as ends, not as means. Machiavelli recognizes that there are occasions when a ruler must act cruelly against one person or group of people in order to establish fear as a deterrent against lawlessness, for example.

* Kant thinks one should legislate for a kingdom of ends. Machiavelli knows that treating people as ends in themselves might well lead to anarchy and chaos.

Let us look at just a little of Machiavelli's advice. Here, for example, are his words to a ruler who has taken over a state, but it might equally apply to a managing director who has taken over an ailing company, or a politician inheriting a new ministry.

So it should be noted that when he seizes a state the new ruler ought to determine all the injuries that he will need to inflict. He should inflict them once for all, and not have to renew them every day, and in that way he will be able to set men's minds at rest, and win them over to him when he confers benefits. Whoever acts otherwise, either through timidity

or bad advice, is always forced to have the knife ready in his
hand and he can never depend on his subjects because they,
suffering fresh and continuous violence, can never feel secure
with regard to him. Violence should be inflicted once for
all; people will then forget what it tastes like and so be less
resentful. Benefits should be conferred gradually; and in that
way they will taste better.

(*The Prince*, section VIII)

Like a surgeon, forced in some extreme circumstances to
operate without anaesthetic, one is sometimes in a position where
the inflicting of pain is inevitable and ultimately beneficial.

It might seem irrelevant to ask 'Am I prepared for everyone to
operate without anaesthetics?' because clearly the actual decision
is not based on a general theory but on the immediate and unique
situation. The surgeon might say 'This is not how I would choose
to act, but in the circumstances it is right for me to do so.' What
Machiavelli is saying (and using a utilitarian argument to justify
it) is that less harm will be done by decisive action, than by a
compassionate but indecisive muddle.

And here the advice to a ruler might be adapted for a new
teacher, taking over an unruly class:

So a prince should not worry if he incurs reproach for his
cruelty so long as he keeps his subjects united and loyal. By
making an example or two he will prove more compassionate
than those who, being too compassionate, allow disorders
which lead to murder and rapine. These nearly always harm
the whole community, whereas executions ordered by a
prince only affect individuals.

(*The Prince*, section XVIII)

He acknowledges the traditional virtues, but comments:

... taking everything into account, he (the prince) will find
that some of the things that appear to be virtues will, if he
practises them, ruin him, and some of the things that appear
to be wicked will bring him security and prosperity.

(*The Prince*, section XV)

Now this is not to dismiss entirely the idea that a ruler should do good, merely that a ruler should be flexible enough to recognize that it is not always prudent.

> *... he should have a flexible disposition, varying as fortune and circumstances dictate. As I said above, he should not deviate from what is good, if that is possible, but he should know how to do evil, if that is necessary.*

(*The Prince*, section XVIII)

For our purposes, there are four features of Machiavelli's advice that we may need to take into account:

* In many situations, traditional virtues may be set aside, and actions judged on a utilitarian basis. Keeping order and minimizing pain take precedence over traditional moral principles.
* Actions depend on the duties and responsibilities of the position you hold in society. A prince might be justified, therefore, in doing something that would not be acceptable in one of his subjects. Once you have accepted the position of ruler, you are obliged to seek the benefit and integrity of the state – your morality in other respects being subsumed beneath that overall obligation. Morality is therefore related to social position.
* In practical terms, one needs to be flexible, adapting moral principles to suit particular situations.
* What we do should depend on our awareness of the likely actions and attitudes of those around us. If everyone else were good, there would be no problem – but they are not, and so we remain naively innocent at our own peril.

There is, of course, an answer to Machiavelli, but it is not an easy one. One could say: 'I will do what I know to be right, no matter what the consequences, to myself, my family and friends, my country. I will not compromise my integrity, however much pain that might cause.' That is a valid moral position to take, for someone who holds his or her principles very dear. Martyrs take such a stand.

Let Machiavelli stand for those who are sceptical about the application of moral principles. This is not a total scepticism about moral values – which implies that there are no values other than those that individuals choose to impose on life – it is just scepticism about the application of general rules to individual situations.

Situation ethics

In the 1960s, largely as a reaction against what he saw as a paternalistic and imposed morality of traditional Christianity, Joseph Fletcher developed **situation ethics**.

He argued against the deductive method of ethics (in which you start with a rule or principle, and then apply it to various particular cases), and suggested that the individual situation should be paramount. He believed that there should be **a single moral principle – that you should do whatever is the most loving thing**. Ethical rules were of secondary importance; they might guide a person, but should not dictate right and wrong.

The requirement to do the most loving thing is not a rule or law – it does not say *what* you should do in any particular situation – it merely gives a motive and attitude that can inform moral choice. Of course, a person may act foolishly out of love, with disastrous consequences, but nevertheless, from a strictly situationist ethical perspective, it is still morally right. Each situation is taken and judged by what love requires, and if that means breaking some conventional moral rule, it is right to do so.

Situation ethics, in putting individual circumstances before fixed moral rules, nevertheless accepted one absolute principle: love. But what if there is no absolute principle that can be applied to all situations? This leads us to the general issue of relativism.

Relativism and moral absolutes

Any **absolutist** approach to ethics is going to argue that it is possible to find a basic feature of the world, human nature, biology or pure reason on which a system of ethics can be built. Once that foundation is established, moral principles and the right or wrong of particular actions can follow by logical deduction and practical application.

That is not to imply that absolutist ethics is inflexible; all moral systems need to take some account of particular circumstances, intentions and so on. However, every absolutist ethic is based on something other than itself, some reality or shared value, by which it is justified. Looking at the ethical theories we have considered so far:

* Natural law ethics is based on a rational interpretation of purpose within a rationally comprehensible universe.
* Virtue ethics is based on an understanding of the essence of what it is to be a mature human being, and the virtues that spring from that.
* Utilitarianism is based on the assumption that a rational person (whether from altruism or enlightened self-interest) will want a democratic sharing out of benefits.
* Kant based his ethics on the pure practical reason and the logical application of his categorical imperative.
* Even where personal development, whether with a fixed idea of the self or an evolutionary one, is used as a basis for ethics, it is based on an ideal of what a person can become and understands morality in the light of that.

This does not imply that any of these are 'absolutist' in any narrow sense, but it does show that they all depend on some prior commitment or understanding, by which right and wrong can be judged.

Relativism also starts with a couple of basic assumptions, but they are very different from any of those listed above. It assumes:

* that the only absolute rule is that there are no absolute rules
* that nobody should impose his or her morality on anyone else.

Early in this book (see Chapter 2) we made the distinction between descriptive and normative ethics. The former simply described what people do in particular situations, without attempting to label that behaviour either right or wrong. The latter – which then became the subject matter of all that followed, was concerned with defining and understanding moral norms. Descriptive ethics is relativist. In other words, if you say 'people in such and such a tribe practise cannibalism' you are not making a judgement about whether cannibalism is right or wrong, you are simply noting that it is socially acceptable in that tribe.

What a relativist approach to ethics is doing is extending descriptive ethics into the territory that was previously held by normative ethics. In other words, it argues that all issues of right and wrong should be seen as culturally, socially and temporally conditioned. We should not take moral norms or rules from one society and impose them on another; nor should we assume that the rules that applied in one era can be continued into another.

Those who argue for any of the traditional ethical systems tend to regard relativism as a dangerous medicine; taken in small quantities it is useful (in warning against too rigid an application of ethical maxims), but overdoses can be fatal – in the sense that they tend to preclude the rational discussion of genuine differences of opinion.

applied ethics

During the first half of the twentieth century, philosophers were mainly concerned with meta-ethics, exploring what it meant to make a moral statement, but were not expected to engage directly in debating moral issues. That situation has changed dramatically during the last fifty years. The anti-war movements of the 1960s and 1970s, the contraceptive pill, the sexual revolution, feminism, environmental issues, global warming, terrorism and financial crises have all thrust ethics to the fore.

Ethical theories only come alive when they are applied to real-life situations and used to inform moral choice. The range of applied ethics today is huge: environmental ethics, gender issues, sexuality, equality and fairness across economic, racial or religious divides, business ethics, medical and nursing ethics, professional ethics, media ethics.

In this chapter we select just four topics – the natural environment, animal rights, warfare and abortion – in order to show something of the way in which ethical theories may be applied.

The natural environment

We have to recognize that the human species, both by its numbers and its technology, has a massive impact on the environment. Yet, until recently, almost all moral thinking focused on human happiness of benefit; directly so in the case of utilitarianism, indirectly in the natural law arguments or the categorical imperative. The tendency has been to seek human flourishing first of all, and to consider other species or other elements in the natural environment only insofar as they impact on humans.

A stone cannot feel pain, or express a preference; therefore, it has traditionally been ignored in moral debates. From a utilitarian point of view, the environment (and other species living within it) has too often only been seen as a moral issue when its destruction threatens to harm humankind.

This approach tends to be short sighted, however, since we are not able to assess the full impact of, for example, climate change on the human species, quite apart from the question of any moral responsibility towards other species or the natural environment for its own sake.

Example

If rainforests are destroyed, we may be concerned because:
* climate change will affect us all
* many medicines are discovered through analysis of rare plant species, many of which are still to be found in the rainforests.

In both cases, this reflects a narrowly utilitarian argument. It does not imply any responsibility towards the rainforest in itself, nor to the other species who live in it.

A second approach is implied by what has already been said about the 'natural law' argument. Whether backed by religious convictions or not, there may be a sense that everything – humans, other species, the planet itself – has its place within an overall scheme of things, a 'final cause' that is its natural destiny. This approach is based on metaphysics, in that it goes beyond descriptions of the physical environment to consider issues of value, meaning and the fundamental structures of reality. It may conclude that the world and its many species should be valued, quite apart from any specific or demonstrable benefit to humankind.

For reflection

The human population is about 6.8 billion and is set to rise to more than 9 billion by 2050. The planet cannot sustain such growth in a species that has such a significant impact on the environment. Whatever is done by way of ethically responsible lifestyle changes in order to reduce the 'human environmental footprint' (in other words, the impact of each person on the planet) it remains true that the only way to reduce a person's footprint to zero is for him or her not to be born! We immediately move on to issues of contraception, population control, social provision, education and so on – all of which impact on the birth rate. And once you do that, moral arguments from a 'natural law' perspective (opposing contraception, for example) start to come into play, to be balanced against a utilitarian assessment of future suffering due to an unsustainable population.

Whether arguing from a utilitarian or natural law basis, it is clear that lifestyle options have a direct impact on the environment. Those concerned to preserve the ecosystems on which life depends, need to make a case for changes in our attitudes to those things that most people take for granted as part of an affluent lifestyle.

Action on climate change

The climate change summit held in Copenhagen in December 2009 failed to achieve any legally binding agreements to lower carbon emissions, to the frustration of most of those involved. While accepting the scientific evidence for the impact of global warming on the future of the planet, and recognizing that something needs to be done to restrain the rise in temperatures, all that the summit achieved was a general statement of intent.

There were many complex political and economic issues standing in the way of an agreement, but in terms of ethics, the problem lay in conflicting utilitarian calculations. On the one hand, there is the long-term benefit to the planet of binding agreements to ensure the reduction of the human contribution to climate change. On the other, is the need for political leaders to calculate the benefits sought by their people in a world where nations compete against one another. In the end, national self-interest (and thus the satisfaction of the preferences of a majority of people in each country) seemed to take precedence over the preference of the global community.

When Rawls argued for justice as fairness he required those who came to decide on the principles of justice to forget who they were. The problem is, in the real world, those who come together to take decisions that affect the whole globe simply cannot forget where they come from or whom they represent.

Animal rights

So far, everything we have been considering has been concerned with the way in which human beings treat one another, but humankind is just one of many species on this planet, so we need to ask if the sort of moral considerations that have been applied to the treatment of other human beings should be extended to include other species.

This does not imply that animals should behave morally – without reason, morality makes no sense. A cat, offered the prospect of killing a mouse, acts instinctively, but (as we shall consider in a moment) humans can choose how they will behave towards other species.

But do we as a species have any moral obligations towards other species? Do animals have rights – and, if so, how are those rights assessed? Let us look at the way in which some ethical arguments might be applied to animals.

In practical terms, we may want to ask:

* Is it right to keep wild animals caged in zoos?
* Is the concept of making an animal into a 'pet' one that damages its original nature?
* Should we breed favourite species on grounds of aesthetic appeal?

Fairness

Ethical theories that are based on the idea of a social contract drawn up between people are concerned with the fairness within a relationship. Each party accepts responsibilities and in return receives rights. Can this sort of theory be applied to other species?

A pet is accepted into a human social setting for the benefit of the humans. For example, looking after a pet hamster may be a way of encouraging children to take responsibility generally, as well as giving them pleasure. A dog or cat may be good company, especially for people living on their own. A family pet may be thought to offer something positive to the life and atmosphere of a family home. A relationship develops between the pet animal and the humans, through expressions of affection and shared enjoyments (like dog and owner taking walks together).

In what way does the animal benefit from this arrangement? By being given food and shelter, veterinary care and all else needed, to enable it to live out its natural lifespan in a measure of comfort seldom offered in its natural habitat?

Where animals are treated cruelly, once accepted into the human environment, then it is clear that the humans have not acted fairly in terms of the implied contract between themselves and the animal.

In other words, if you accept a pet, you have a moral responsibility to care for it in a way that is appropriate to its needs. That is only fair, according to the implied contract you have with it. You may be prosecuted for inhumane treatment on that basis.

Natural law

It might be argued that humans have no right to be entering into such implied contracts with animals. The Islamic view of life, for example, is that animals should not be kept as pets or put into zoos. It regards this as basically unnatural, and therefore as violating the natural life and instincts of the animal. In this case, the argument being used is one of 'natural law'; that animals have their natural place within the scheme of things, and are not to be treated as pets. Respect for the animal demands that it should be treated as an animal, not as a quasi-human, manicured, clipped and paraded!

On the other hand, animals in the wild feed on one another. Humans are omnivorous, and therefore have a choice – they can either eat animals or remain vegetarian. A natural law argument might well accept that there is a place for the eating of meat, and therefore also for the farming of animals. But if the eating of meat in order to sustain life is justified under natural law, what about the conditions in which the farming of animals takes place? Most species do not have any choice about their feeding habits; they simply catch what they can. The human species, on the other hand, controls the production of animals for food. Does such control imply moral responsibility?

Example

A cat will play with, kill and eat a mouse. The sight of this might be extremely distasteful, but it is a cat's nature to do so. However much the cat may have been domesticated, it is still a natural hunter with killer instincts. On the other hand, if I decide to take a pet mouse out of its cage, set it free in a room and then chase after it, biting it from time to time before killing and eating it, I would be considered to be acting in a way that is unnatural, and the morality of having such a supper would be questioned. My feeding habits might feature in a tabloid newspaper, and I might find myself under pressure to accept psychotherapy. I would certainly be banned from keeping pet mice.

* What distinguishes me from the cat in this respect?
* Does my rationality and ability to choose other sources of food mean that I have a moral responsibility towards the mouse?

If I were starving, would I be morally justified in eating the mouse?

The treatment of animals is connected with questions about diet and standards of living. If fresh meat is enjoyed occasionally, and a roast chicken is regarded as a delicacy, it becomes more possible to breed chickens in humane circumstances – fewer are needed and people will pay more for what is considered a delicacy. On the other hand, if people expect to eat meat every day, the demand goes up and artificial methods are found to maximize the efficiency of meat production. A change in eating habits and expectations therefore implies a change in attitude to animals, even aside from the issue of vegetarianism.

How do you assess the fairness of an implied contract in which a member of one species is born, reared and fattened, and then killed to feed members of another species? All the gains would seem to be on one side. The animal used for food is not considered as an individual member of a species, but simply as a source of protein.

Natural law sees everything – and therefore every species – as having a place within the overall scheme of things within the universe. Hence animals are regarded as having significance, but not the same significance as human beings, since they have a very different essence. Where a metaphysics is evolutionary, or emphasizes the interrelationship between all life forms – for example within Buddhism – the welfare of one species is bound up with the welfare of others, and the treatment of animals is therefore most definitely a moral concern.

Experiments on animals

Animal rights activists target laboratories that conduct experiments on animals – and tend to do so irrespective of the purpose of the research being undertaken. In other words, they oppose the use of animals in this way, whether the aim is to find a cure for a serious human disease or whether it is to test cosmetics. In this, they are rejecting a utilitarian approach.

Using a utilitarian argument, the gains to be anticipated must outweigh the pain inflicted. Thus, if it is possible to use an animal in a test that might result in a cure for a serious disease, then many people would judge that a morally acceptable thing to do. Of course, it would need to be shown that as little suffering as possible was inflicted on the animals concerned. On the other hand, the testing of cosmetics on animals does not yield life-saving benefits. Cosmetics are not essential to life. The use of cosmetics that have been tested on animals is therefore optional, a matter of personal moral choice. One teenager, campaigning for the use of cruelty-free cosmetics, used the slogan 'Make up your mind before you make up your face' to highlight the nature of the choice involved.

Therefore, using a combination of a natural respect for the life of animals and a utilitarian approach to the expected gains from experimentation, the main moral questions about animal experimentation may be set out as:

* Is it necessary to use animals in these tests, or is there some other way to obtain the same information?
* Are the tests carried out in such a way as to minimize the pain caused?
* Are the anticipated results of the tests of sufficient importance to justify the suffering involved?

The rights and needs of animals

The Australian philosopher Peter Singer is particularly well known for his work on the ethics of our treatment of animals – although he is influential across the whole area of applied ethics. His approach is utilitarian, in other words he wants to consider the happiness or benefit of all concerned. Unlike earlier utilitarians, however, he sees no reason why the argument should be limited to humans. Just because animals cannot express their preferences, it does not follow that the benefit or harm caused to them should not be taken into account in a utilitarian assessment. In his view, any creature that is capable of feeling pain deserves to have its needs taken into consideration.

> Singer argues that, just as we now recognize that sexism and racism are wrong, so we should avoid 'speciesism' – giving privileged or exclusive consideration to the needs or preferences of the human species to the exclusion of all others.

In general, the argument of the animal rights movement – and others who want to consider the welfare of animals without considering themselves to be part of a campaign or movement – is that other species should be considered as worthy of consideration in themselves, and not used as the property of human beings. Hence, for example, some would argue that just as liberty and protection from the threat of cruel treatment is regarded as basic to the rights of a human being, so they should be extended to animals.

Just as, in any preference utilitarian argument, we need to look at the particular situation and needs of the people involved, so we may need to consider what rights are appropriate for each particular species. Part of that may be a consideration of those things that animals seek in order to live and reproduce. An example (given by James Rachels in *Can Ethics Provide Answers?*) is that of a bird building a nest. Clearly, if we watch a bird build a nest and then take that nest away, or deliberately destroy it, we are depriving that bird of something that it needs, and it will have to start building all over again. Similarly, if another bird takes over a nest that is already built, we might tend to see that as unjust. Hence, by looking at the needs of a bird, we might conclude that the right to gain benefit from a nest that it has built would seem to be a fairly clear right. And that amounts to giving property rights to the bird, since the bird has invested effort in taking twigs (nominally the property of nobody and everybody) and investing energy and skill in constructing a property out of them.

This is further reflected in the fact that it is illegal to steal and sell rare birds eggs. A species of bird is deemed to have the right to reproduce itself, and that right is taken away if its eggs are stolen.

In this way, one can build up a case for some basic rights, appropriate to the essential needs of each species, the upholding of which will allow that species to survive and have the opportunity to flourish.

Unfortunately for those concerned about animal welfare, there are some today who might still follow the line taken by the eighteenth-century philosopher Immanuel Kant, who said:

> *But so far as animals are concerned, we have no direct duties. Animals are not self-conscious, and they are merely as means to an end. That end is man.*

(from *Lectures on Ethics*, quoted by Rachels
in *Can Ethics Provide Answers?*, p. 100)

That is a classic example of what Singer calls 'speciesism', but it is in line with Kant's moral theory – namely that he wants to consider human beings as autonomous and rational ends in themselves. We have already seen the difficulty of applying Kant's principles in a world where people do not behave rationally. That applies equally to a world in which sentient and sensitive beings happen to belong to other species and are therefore unable to have a rational discussion with us!

War and peace

War is the most destructive of all human activities – not just in terms of the loss of life and the damage done to the infrastructure of a country, but in the broader sense that war takes away the basic security that enables civilization to continue, for civilization depends on security and peace. Ethical issues arise whenever peace is threatened by an act of aggression, and, in general, actions are deemed 'just' or 'right' if they aim to re-establish peace and justice. But if a just peace can only be secured by the use or threat of violence, does that make it right?

It is not surprising then that there is an ongoing debate about the ethics of war, and this section will try to outline just a few of the key issues. The debate centres on a number of questions:

* When, if at all, is it right to go to war?
* Who has the right to declare war? A single nation? The UN?
* How should wars be fought, if they cannot be avoided?

* Is any one form of weapon inherently morally better than another?
* Is the use (or even the possession) of weapons of mass destruction ever justified ethically?
* How do you distinguish terrorism from warfare?
* Is it possible to guard against terrorism and warfare without eroding either civil liberties or the right of nations to self-determination?

And behind these questions are others relating to the relationship between individuals, minority groups and nations, where these give rise to conflicting loyalties. There is also the question of religion, and how that relates to the divisions between or within nations.

The 'just war' theory

The starting point here is whether, and in what circumstances, a war can be considered just. There are two categories of issues here:
* Those concerned with the right to go to war (jus ad bellum).
* Those concerned with the way in which a war should be fought (jus in bello).

The principles for this were set out by Thomas Aquinas in the thirteenth century, but with later developments. A just war approach would argue that:

1 It may be just to go to war if:
   * It is done by proper authority (e.g. by a nation, not by an individual. Can a terrorist group be a 'proper authority'? And what of 'state-sponsored' terrorism – if the group has the backing of one or more sovereign states, would that make the act a valid act of war?)
   * There is a good reason to go to war (e.g. in self-defence. But does that give a nation the right to a pre-emptive strike against another, for example on the basis of intelligence that suggests the other is in possession of weapons of mass destruction?)
   * The intention of going to war is to establish peace and justice (in other words, war should not become an end in itself, but only a means of restoring justice).

2 The conduct of war is considered right only if:
  * It is waged against military personnel, not against civilians. (But is it ever possible to wage war without civilian casualties, either directly or indirectly? Can 'smart weapons', which claim to minimize 'collateral' damage, be seen as more acceptable morally? What about the economic harm and further suffering that civilians face even when the war is over?)
  * The force used is proportional. (In other words, the harm likely to be caused by an action should not outweigh what that action sets out to gain. It is very difficult to judge this, but an example of its failure might be the huge loss of life in some of the battles of the First World War, for a negligible gain.)
  * Minimum force is used in order to achieve one's end (which would preclude the use of all weapons of mass destruction, or excessive conventional force against a lightly defended target).

Those who go against the accepted norms of warfare may be accused of crimes against humanity if, for example, they deliberately set out to kill civilians. Here the issue is intention; was that killing the accidental consequence of military action or its deliberate aim? In other words, if civilians are killed because a bomb fails to hit its intended military target, does this have the same moral force as the deliberate disregard for civilian life? In weighing up such things, we need to ask if sufficient care was taken by those planning the attack, and so on.

In terms of the ethical principles that underlie the conduct of war, there are two basic lines of argument. One is conformity to agreed statements about rights and responsibilities in the conduct of war. An example of this would be the Geneva Conventions about the treatment of those military personnel who are captured in war, prohibiting torture and so on. The other approach is to use a utilitarian assessment – whether it is the overall aim of a war, or the use of a particular weapon, there is a balance between what it is hoped to gain (e.g. ending the war sooner, restoring justice, saving the lives of other military or civilians) against the destruction and loss of life involved.

Terrorism

In general, acts of terrorism are condemned on a 'just war' theory, even if those carrying them out claim that their cause is just, because:

* They are not backed by legitimate authority. (But should a nation state constitute that authority, or the United Nations? Can a religion constitute valid authority?)
* They are generally (but not always) aimed at causing civilian casualties as a means of influencing public and political opinion.

In a war situation, the invading nation has a responsibility to restore peace to the country it invades. Failure to take proper steps to manage the aftermath of war detracts from any moral validity in conducting that war in the first place. With terrorism, this is simply not possible.

There is a fundamental problem with historical perspectives on this. Yesterday's terrorist may, in retrospect, be seen as a freedom fighter and become an ally. This is particularly significant where terrorism has been limited (or has attempted to limit itself) to attacks on military personnel or other representatives of the state, rather than on the civilian population. Hence, the terrorist of today may see his or her action as an expression of a struggle that will one day vindicate the acts of terror.

The standard counter to such an argument is that all other methods to restore justice should have been exhausted before resorting to violence, which is seldom the case. However, it is asking a great deal of people who are being oppressed that they should continue indefinitely to press for peaceful means of change.

But even if all other means of bringing about change have been tried and failed, it is still far from clear how you establish a utilitarian justification of violence in terms of its long-term results. The terrorist might claim that his or her action will, in the long run, contribute to an overall justice and will therefore be justified. Others will argue that the intended end result, however just in itself, cannot be used to justify acts that deliberately cause suffering to the innocent.

Weaponry

All weapons which by their nature and method of use are likely to cause civilian casualties, are not a proportionate response to a threat or do not represent minimum necessary force, may be deemed wrong. In the extreme case, the use of weapons of mass destruction (i.e. nuclear, chemical and biological weapons), which by their nature cause widespread damage and loss of life, cannot be justified. The only justification for holding such weapons is deterrence. On the other hand, conventional weapons, used inappropriately (e.g. the systematic bombing of cities) can have the same devastating effect as weapons of mass destruction, and can therefore be condemned on the same basis.

Smart weapons are designed to destroy their pre-selected targets and minimize collateral damage. Is a smart weapon inherently more moral than one that kills in a less well targeted way, or that causes more civilian casualties? Clearly, from a utilitarian standpoint it is, since it aims to minimise suffering. But that does not imply that the use of the weapon is right in itself – the situation may be one in which it is wrong to use any weapon, smart or otherwise.

The beginning and end of life

If ethics is concerned with examining moral issues that relate to the rights and responsibilities of individuals and to the value of human life that are implied by them, it is understandable that all matters related to choosing when life should begin and when it should end, are going to be of particular importance. Ethics is most sharply focused when it is a matter of life or death, whether that is at the beginning or end of the human lifespan.

Abortion

Of all the ethical issues people face today, abortion is probably the one that most clearly illustrates the contrasting bases on which moral judgements are made. The facts are not in doubt, the arguments have been presented time and again, and yet there is no consensus view.

The issue of abortion can be approached logically, pragmatically, or from the standpoint of the personal, physical and emotional needs of the woman who seeks the abortion. It can be seen as an intensely personal issue, or one that is a touchstone for the protection of human rights throughout society. Abortion may be seen on one side as a woman's right, and on the other as the first step towards compulsory euthanasia, selective breeding and wholesale denial of the uniqueness and rights of each human person.

British law requires that the agreement of two doctors be given for a pregnancy to be terminated. Abortion can be legally permitted if the foetus is seriously defective, if the risk to the health of the mother from having the child is considered greater than the risk of the termination, and if the birth of the child would have a seriously damaging effect on the mother, taking into account the psychological and social situation of the mother and other members of the family.

Abortions can take place (according to British law) up to 24 weeks after conception. However, they can be performed after that if there is a risk that the mother will be permanently injured by continuing with the pregnancy, or if the child is seriously handicapped.

An anti-abortion argument

Both the ancient Greeks and Romans killed weak or deformed babies by exposing them to the elements. This was justified ethically by both Plato and Aristotle, on the grounds that death was to be preferred to a stunted life.

Christianity opposed this, on the grounds that each person had an eternal soul, and was made in the image of God. The decision about when a person should die was to be left to God alone. The crucial question is: When does human life start? If the foetus has a 'soul' then it should be protected.

St Augustine thought that the foetus was 'animated' (received its soul) 60 or 80 days after conception. English law originally followed this principle, and distinguished between abortions before and after 'quickening' – the time when a mother might feel the movement of the child within her.

In the UK (following the 1990 Human Fertilization and Embryology Act), the age limit for abortions was lowered to 24 weeks (except in exceptional circumstances, where the health of the mother is seriously threatened). In the USA, the Supreme Court decision of 1973 set the time limit for abortions at six months.

The general recognition here is that it is wrong to kill a foetus if it is capable of surviving independently. At this point, it receives the right of protection as a separate human being. The point made by the anti-abortionists is that such right of protection should be extended back to the earliest stages of conception.

It could be argued that many pregnancies are terminated naturally, which might make an abortion an 'elected miscarriage', and that therefore there is no reason why an individual foetus should be protected. But this argument is not logical. Human beings are being killed naturally all the time. If I stab someone through the heart, I cannot plead in my defence that many people suffer sudden cardiac arrest, and that I am simply electing that the person should die in that particular way. To induce a cardiac arrest is an action for which I would be morally responsible. To terminate the life of a foetus is also an action for which moral responsibility should be taken, irrespective of whether or not nature might have done the same thing.

Those who oppose abortion also point out that, once life is devalued at one particular point, then all life is under threat. They may present abortion as a touchstone for assessing issues like involuntary euthanasia, or even eugenics (selective breeding). Once the principle is established that it is legally and morally acceptable to destroy life in one particular case, then life in general is threatened.

The pro-freedom argument

This argument is not presented as pro-abortion, because very few people would actually choose to have an abortion. It is not regarded as a 'good' to be sought, but rather as the lesser of two evils. The argument is about who should decide whether an abortion is to be carried out.

Those who say that a woman should be free to decide whether or not to have an abortion generally do so on two grounds:

* That the foetus is essentially part of a woman's body until it is capable of independent life, and that the potential mother herefore has total moral right to do what she wishes with her potential offspring, simply because, at this stage, the life is seen as potential, rather than actual.

* That giving birth to children should be seen in terms of the overall situation in which a woman finds herself. She should be free to decide that her own personal development will be stunted by continuing with the pregnancy, or that the financial and social circumstances into which the child would be born would be such, that perhaps the whole family might suffer as a result.

In part, this argument is utilitarian – weighing the loss of the potential life now against the benefits to the mother and others. In utilitarian terms, those who justify abortion generally use an **act utilitarian** approach, whereas the anti-abortionists use a **rule utilitarian** approach. Even where benefits in this particular situation appear to go in favour of abortion, a rule utilitarian view might be that the right to destroy life in one situation threatens life everywhere, and that the greater good is achieved by giving all life a chance to develop.

Arguments about abortion may therefore involve all the forms of ethical justification so far outlined. Natural law is used to protect the unborn child; utilitarianism in both forms is used to assess the result of the abortion, personal development and the freedom of an individual in a 'right to choose' argument.

Because women are so intimately involved with the process of conception, pregnancy, birth and child-rearing, the ethical discussion of abortion tends to highlight other issues in terms of women's rights and their role in society.

Some conclusions

Moral progress: illusion or necessary hope?

We live in a world of change; everything evolves, nothing is fixed. Whether we look at the evolution of species or the changes happening in society, we try to make sense of change as though it were a story, and ask about the ending. Faced with change or development we tend to ask 'Where is it going?' Progress – as opposed to random or circular change – implies a direction and an end point.

History is always a story told from a particular perspective; facts in themselves do not make history. In the same way, descriptive ethics – the catalogue of who does what in what society and during what era – does not touch on the fundamental issues of normative ethics. It does not ask if society is 'better' now than in Greek, Roman or Medieval times. We may not burn witches, but do we still torture? Is the freedom to be openly homosexual a return to the enlightened times of the Greek city state, recovering from a temporary period of unfair repression? Is there a new world order emerging, or is universal communication merely giving the opportunity for people to exploit more widely?

If facts alone cannot make a normative moral argument, then facts alone cannot prove that there is moral progress. Hence, any attempt to prove moral progress will hit the same problem that utilitarianism finds – that there is no end point at which all the evidence is in and we can make a definitive judgement. At that level, moral progress remains an illusion, never unambiguously proved or demonstrated.

And yet ... If there were no sense of progress, of trying to improve a situation or cultivate a virtue, would the sense of right and wrong continue? Is having a conscience compatible with an absence of hope or any sense of what a better life could be?

The art of living as a human being involves thinking, creating, hoping, willing; it is always oriented towards the future. We may look back, but we live forwards.

Without any hope that morality makes sense, the very experience of morality becomes nonsense. In this sense, moral progress is a necessary hope – for without it, the rest of moral discussion loses its significance. There may be no evidence whatsoever that things are improving. But in the face of that bleakness, the moral impulse is to want to make it so – to construct a life according to our intuitions of what is right.

Progress is therefore a bit like freedom; analyse it empirically and it vanishes. I am utterly determined by events beyond my control, and yet I sense that I am free to choose what to do. **In the same way, I have no evidence of progress, but the experience of morality is of constructing a better situation and therefore of willing progress.**

So where does this leave us?

The moral choices people make are based on many things, but they are rooted in an understanding of the nature of the world, and the values that arise from that understanding. For some people this is well thought out and rational; for others it is provided by a religion and accepted ready made; others act instinctively, their understanding and valuation of the world working through their unconscious.

In the broadest sense, this is metaphysics: the quest to understand the meaning and value of the world as a whole. This is the process that lay behind the 'natural law' arguments, but it can be broader than the world view of Aristotle on which that theory was based.

The moment of moral choice is therefore informed by the way in which we generally understand and value life. Iris Murdoch expressed it in this way:

We act rightly 'When the time comes' not out of strength of will but out of a quality of our usual attachments and with the

> *kind of energy and discernment which we have available. And to this the whole activity of our consciousness is relevant.*
>
> (Iris Murdoch, *The Sovereignty of Good*, 1970, p. 53)

To ask 'What should I do?' implies the question 'What is life for?' Life is constantly changing; nothing, not even our galaxy, remains fixed. We can try to run from this truth – craving absolutes that will justify our decisions for all time – but it is an illusion. Constant change is a reality, and it affects not just the world around us, but ourselves. We are not fixed as individuals, our minds shape the future; the choices we make today define the sort of people we become tomorrow.

We also have to accept that life, however much we shape it to suit our own ends, involves suffering and death. We can work to minimize suffering and promote happiness, but we cannot remove the fact that humans are limited and fragile creatures. Fallibility and failure are not just accidental features of life that should be quickly removed and forgotten; they are a feature of living in this sort of world, in which human aspirations outstrip human abilities.

Every choice we make is informed by many things – hopes, fears, the things we value and the understanding of life that we have gathered through education, the influence of others and personal experience. Whether we recognize this consciously or not, the act of making a moral choice sums up all that we have become.

The relationship between ethical arguments and the moral life is rather like that between literary theory and the creative writer, or between musical theory and the act of composition. Writer and composer use all their feelings, intuitions, values and insights to produce a work of art that is unique. Later, the theorists and critics may analyse it, place it in within categories or the development of a particular style, or reveal likely influences.

Ethics is rather like that. It analyses moral choices and devises theories to show how they may be justified. It is a valuable process, a useful guide for future action, but it can never fully explain or adequately legislate for the process of creative living.